She Said,
He Said

conversation. Gender differences as revealed by survey responses are fun to look at and talk about. Many people still agree with the sentiment "*Vive la difference,*" finding the opposite sex's habits, beliefs, and pronouncements interesting, if not strange. *She Said, He Said* shows both the fun and serious side of the gender gap.

For example, changes in two of America's cherished institutions—marriage and the work place—are tracked over the last two decades. Demographic data from the survey shows that divorce rates have risen and that many of those who opt for marriage and family are making those choices much later in life (probably as a response to having seen others go through divorce or opting for career moves early in their adulthood). Those who marry and stay married are experiencing lower levels of satisfaction within the bonded state; what's the cause?

What's So Important About Opinion Data?

Opinion data support much of the recent media concern that male/female relations in this country need some work. Obvious differences exist between the sexes; they look and act quite distinct from one another. If we ignore these differences we cannot hope to succeed in enlisting the other gender's help in redressing our grievances and solving our problems.

Which would be too bad, because television is not all that entertaining these days.

Most of all, solutions to problems should respect the dignity of both sexes. Sometimes one sex's approach to a problem or its best solution unwittingly denigrates the other sex. How many judges have insulted the whole female population by suggesting that because a woman was out after dark, her rapist was somehow less culpable? By the same token, solving the child abduction problem by hammering it into children that all men are to be feared is unfair. It alienates men from any protective role in the community, and leaves many innocent men feeling as much of a pariah as the child molester. True solutions must be in the interest of the whole society, the family, and both partners in a relationship, and cannot ignore long-term ramifications for either of the genders.

Whence The Data?

The statistical data for *She Said, He Said* is derived from a massive reference work entitled *An American Profile—Opinions and Behavior, 1972-1989,* edited by Floris Wood. This 1,100-page work displays a more wide-ranging set of data by total population, race, and age in addition to gender.

Published by Gale Research Inc., *An American Profile* is likely to be available in the reference collection of most medium or large-sized public libraries.

The survey instrument that gathers the data used in both *She Said, He Said* and *An American Profile* is the General Social Survey (GSS) conducted by the National Opinion Research Center (NORC) at the University of Chicago.

This collection of data should be declared a national treasure. Gathered every year except 1979 and 1981, the GSS data have been available to the research community for several years. Countless articles, newspaper columns, TV soundbites, and books have resulted. The General Social Survey is highly esteemed by researchers not only for the survey's longevity but also for its accuracy and dependability.

For instance, in 1979 and 1981, not enough funds were available to guarantee a survey that met the usual high standards set by the NORC. Rather than compromise the quality of the survey by using cheaper telephone or mail-in techniques instead of high quality face-to-face interviews, the survey was not conducted at all!

Be forewarned: some survey years show a disturbing fluctuation in the response to a question, i.e., a very much higher or lower percent of the population will give a certain response to a question than in previous or subsequent years. Most such anomalies are legitimate, caused by events influencing public opinion. For instance, the ups and downs of the economy; serious crime incidents; or suspected malfeasance on the part of several noted politicians. If the GSS questions are asked a short time after these types of notable incidents, the responses inevitably display a reaction.

The Authors' Disclaimer

The authors' commentary on General Social Survey data in no way constitutes a scientific treatise. Everyone has an opinion; our aim was to provide possibilities and hypothetical situations, sincere yet conscious of the fascination that makes this information so endlessly entertaining.

The wonderful thing with statistics is that they can be interpreted any number of ways. *She Said, He Said* provides you with nearly 20 years of serious numbers and trends that you may contemplate to your heart's content.

INTRODUCTION

Feminine. Masculine. That *yin-yang* thing.

"We are just statistics, born to consume resources," wrote Horace (like Madonna, no last name) some 2,000 years ago.

Opinions. Everybody's got *one*. Every coin has *two* sides.

"There are three kinds of lies: lies, damned lies and statistics," said Benjamin Disraeli.

America is abuzz with change for both women and men. As we leap (stumble?) into the next century, how we work, love, procreate, and recreate are undergoing a metamorphosis. We've been told a lot lately that women think differently from men. And vice versa. That the genders have different styles of communication. That male and female behavior owes much to ingrained social and sexual wiring.

Is this true? we wondered. And if so, how are women and men viewing life these days? Are we becoming more alike or different? Have we changed much since Nixon was president? Or since the days of Ford and Carter? And what did that long decade with Reagan do to us? Armed and curious, *She Said, He Said* takes to the road and asks women and men across America such questions as:

- ☞ What do female and male boomers, 77 million strong with an attitude, believe and how are they changing society?
- ☞ Whatever happened to the sexual revolution? Who won? Are our sex lives any better now than they were 20 years ago? Or are we still watching too much television?
- ☞ Do we like our jobs? Do we work too much? How is the Mommy Track changing corporate America? And what about the newly discovered Daddy Track?
- ☞ How are working women working over the work place? How has working outside the home changed women's satisfaction with family life and life in general? Whatever happened to the housewife and does anybody miss her?

☛ How are women and men faring financially? Who's getting richer? Who's not?

☛ What kind of world will our children inherit? And how are we preparing them for it?

☛ How does race change the attitudes of women and men on key political, economic, and religious issues?

☛ Why is the 18 to 23 age group often referred to as the "Eisenhower generation?" And do they have anything in common with the 66+ set?

☛ Are we happy yet?

These and 100 other questions are answered in *She Said, He Said.* Female and male viewpoints are investigated on a host of issues that really matter. Family. Money. Sex. Politics. Religion. Work. *She Said, He Said* is based on the ground-breaking General Social Survey (GSS), conducted by the respected and well-quoted National Opinion Research Center (NORC) at the University of Chicago. For nearly two decades, researchers have gone door-to-door throughout the country, asking thousands of people hundreds of probing questions.

The female/male statistical tables presented in *She Said, He Said* are just part of the giant GSS information base, which includes statistics on a wide array of topics, measured by total population, race, and age in addition to gender. The population, race, and age data, while not displayed, are often referred to within *She Said, He Said* in order to provide more context for the female and male opinions. For instance, the age groups, organized in nine groups (each with a six-year span except for the 66+), may differ dramatically on any given question, and when that occurs, we will note it. Those groups are 18-23, 24-29, 30-35, 36-41, 42-47, 48-53, 54-59, 60-65, and the 66+.

When interpreting the tables, keep these points in mind as well:

☛ The percentages in the tables are rounded to the nearest whole number.

☛ For various reasons—the size of the GSS questionnaire being one factor—not all questions were asked each year. No survey, for instance, was conducted in 1979 and 1981, due to lack of funding. When years other than 1979 and 1981 are missing, that fact is noted following the question.

☛ Occasionally you may find that the total number of people surveyed in a particular year is about half the number as in previous or later years. NORC has occasionally experimented with a question, rewording it for half of the respondents. No attempt was made to combine the two groups.

In addition to the statistical tables, *She Said, He Said* reports the results from a wide variety of recent polls. The findings from these surveys tend to substantiate or occasionally contradict the GSS data, or they may explore related issues.

What About The Movie?

She Said, He Said bears no relation to the movie of a similar title. The book acquired its title some time before the movie was released, and after seeing the movie, we saw no reason to change it.

Acknowledgments

Several people helped make this book possible, including Tom Clynes, Marie MacNee, and Jenny Lane Sweetland. Appreciation is also extended to Art Chartow, Jeanne Moore, and Sandy Barris. Chris John Miko and Edward Weilant, authors of *Opinions '90*, are thanked as well.

Demographic and Other General Information on Respondents

Who are the respondents and why are they saying these things? Here's some general information on the respondents: their ages, race, jobs, what part of the nation they hail from, and whether they're big city, small town, or something-in-between kind of folk.

Q: **Respondent's age.**

Responses:	18-23	24-29	30-35	36-41	42-47
	48-53	54-59	60-65	66+	

SEX	RESP	'72	'73	'74	'75	'76	'77	'78	'80	'82	'83	'84	'85	'86	'87	'88	'89
F	18-23	9%	11%	11%	12%	10%	11%	12%	12%	9%	8%	9%	8%	8%	9%	9%	8%
	24-29	13	14	15	16	15	13	16	14	15	18	16	15	12	13	14	13
	30-35	13	11	13	12	13	13	14	13	14	15	15	14	15	14	13	14
	36-41	8	12	12	10	11	11	11	9	9	10	12	12	13	13	11	11
	42-47	12	10	11	10	8	9	7	8	8	9	9	8	9	10	10	10
	48-53	11	11	10	10	9	9	7	8	7	7	7	8	7	8	7	9
	54-59	9	11	9	8	8	11	10	8	10	8	7	8	7	6	6	7
	60-65	9	7	7	8	9	8	8	8	9	8	8	8	8	8	8	8
	66+	15	13	14	15	17	15	16	19	18	16	18	20	21	19	22	20
# SURVEYED		803	799	789	815	826	835	883	818	859	905	870	841	844	823	839	873

SEX	RESP	'72	'73	'74	'75	'76	'77	'78	'80	'82	'83	'84	'85	'86	'87	'88	'89
M	18-23	2%	12%	12%	12%	12%	11%	9%	8%	11%	8%	13%	9%	7%	9%	11%	11%
	24-29	16	14	13	15	16	14	17	14	18	18	15	14	18	13	15	13
	30-35	11	11	10	11	11	12	16	17	13	15	12	14	15	16	13	14
	36-41	8	12	9	11	11	11	10	12	11	12	14	12	13	13	16	15
	42-47	11	9	10	10	7	10	9	8	8	9	9	9	10	11	12	11
	48-53	12	9	10	9	8	11	11	9	8	7	7	10	8	10	5	9
	54-59	11	10	10	9	9	10	8	10	9	8	9	9	7	7	6	6
	60-65	8	9	8	7	8	7	6	8	7	9	8	9	8	6	8	6
	66+	2	14	17	16	17	13	14	14	16	13	12	14	14	15	15	16
# SURVEYED		805	701	689	670	667	688	642	641	635	687	597	686	619	638	638	660

Q: What race do you consider yourself?

Responses: W = White   B = Black   O = Other

SEX	RESP	'72	'73	'74	'75	'76	'77	'78	'80	'82	'83	'84	'85	'86	'87	'88	'89
F	W	84%	87%	86%	88%	92%	87%	89%	88%	87%	87%	84%	87%	84%	82%	82%	83%
	B	16	12	13	11	8	13	10	11	11	12	13	10	14	14	13	13
	O	0	1	1	0	0	1	1	1	1	1	3	3	2	3	4	4
# SURVEYED		806	803	793	820	830	837	889	827	867	909	875	846	849	825	843	877

SEX	RESP	'72	'73	'74	'75	'76	'77	'78	'80	'82	'83	'84	'85	'86	'87	'88	'89
M	W	83%	87%	90%	89%	90%	89%	88%	92%	89%	91%	87%	88%	87%	85%	85%	89%
	B	16	12	10	11	9	10	10	7	9	8	9	10	10	11	11	7
	O	0	1	0	0	1	1	1	1	2	1	4	3	3	4	4	4
# SURVEYED		807	701	691	670	669	693	643	641	639	690	598	688	621	641	638	660

Q: Respondent's sex by race.

Race: W = White   B = Black   O = Other
Responses: F = Female   M = Male

SEX	RESP	'72	'73	'74	'75	'76	'77	'78	'80	'82	'83	'84	'85	'86	'87	'88	'89
W	F	50%	53%	53%	55%	56%	54%	58%	55%	57%	56%	58%	55%	57%	56%	56%	55
	M	50	47	47	45	44	46	42	45	43	44	42	45	43	44	44	45
# SURVEYED		1348	1308	1304	1323	1361	1339	1358	1318	1323	1416	1251	1338	1249	1222	1234	1319
B	F	50%	54%	58%	56%	51%	61%	58%	68%	62%	67%	68%	57%	65%	62%	61%	71%
	M	50	46	42	44	49	39	42	32	38	33	32	43	35	38	39	29
SURVEYED		261	183	173	163	129	176	158	140	156	165	170	152	184	191	186	157
O	F	25%	46%	100%	75%	44%	33%	50%	60%	48%	50%	54%	59%	51%	53%	61%	56%
	M	75	54	0	25	56	67	50	40	52	50	46	41	49	47	39	44
SURVEYED		4	13	7	4	9	15	16	10	27	18	52	44	37	53	61	61

Q: Respondent's sex by age group.

Responses: F = Female   M = Male

AGE	RESP	'72	'73	'74	'75	'76	'77	'78	'80	'82	'83	'84	'85	'86	'87	'88	'89
18-23	F	45%	52%	49%	55%	50%	54%	63%	65%	53%	55%	50%	52%	60%	56%	52%	49%
	M	55	48	51	45	50	46	37	35	47	45	50	48	40	44	48	51
# SURVEYED		169	171	168	173	162	164	163	155	148	128	161	133	108	126	141	137
24-29	F	44	54	57	56	53	51	56	56	53	56	60	56	48	55	55	58
	M	56	46	43	44	47	49	44	44	47	44	40	44	52	45	45	42
# SURVEYED		231	212	212	232	226	204	244	202	246	287	232	217	218	193	215	202
30-35	F	54	54	60	56	59	57	54	50	60	56	65	54	58	54	58	56
	M	46	46	40	44	41	43	46	50	40	44	36	46	42	46	42	44
# SURVEYED		187	167	175	171	186	188	230	215	204	236	200	212	221	221	195	212

AGE	RESP	'72	'73	'74	'75	'76	'77	'78	'80	'82	'83	'84	'85	'86	'87	'88	'89
36-41	F	52	53	61	51	55	55	61	49	54	51	54	55	57	56	48	50
	M	48	47	39	49	45	45	39	51	46	49	46	45	43	44	52	50
# SURVEYED		128	175	152	154	158	168	160	150	146	173	187	184	188	186	193	198
42-47	F	51	56	55	55	58	52	50	56	60	59	59	52	56	54	52	56
	M	49	44	45	45	42	48	50	44	40	41	41	48	44	46	48	44
# SURVEYED		186	146	151	143	114	147	119	117	119	145	126	124	141	157	157	161
48-53	F	49	58	51	58	58	50	48	53	54	58	59	50	54	52	62	56
	M	51	42	49	42	42	50	52	47	46	42	41	50	46	48	38	44
# SURVEYED		189	151	146	141	133	154	133	123	112	116	102	131	108	126	92	138

AGE	RESP	'72	'73	'74	'75	'76	'77	'78	'80	'82	'83	'84	'85	'86	'87	'88	'89
54-59	F	46	55	50	53	52	57	64	51	60	57	54	51	58	54	58	60
	M	54	45	50	47	48	43	36	49	40	43	46	49	42	46	42	40
# SURVEYED		156	157	139	126	129	168	137	136	144	134	114	134	99	98	85	99
60-65	F	53	47	50	57	58	56	63	58	64	55	58	53	57	61	59	66
	M	47	53	50	43	42	44	37	42	36	45	42	47	43	39	41	34
# SURVEYED		144	121	108	113	134	117	107	119	116	132	113	131	115	101	119	111
66+	F	57	51	47	54	56	59	62	63	61	62	68	63	67	62	66	63
	M	43	50	53	46	44	41	38	37	39	38	32	37	33	38	34	37
# SURVEYED		218	200	227	232	251	213	232	242	259	241	232	261	265	253	280	275

Q: Geographic region of interview.

SEX	RESP	'72	'73	'74	'75	'76	'77	'78	'80	'82	'83	'84	'85	'86	'87	'88	'89
F	NE	6%	5%	5%	4%	5%	4%	4%	4%	5%	5%	5%	6%	6%	4%	6%	6%
	MA	18	18	18	18	19	16	17	16	17	16	16	14	15	14	15	15
	EN	19	22	22	22	22	23	21	22	21	21	19	17	19	20	18	17
	WN	9	6	6	6	6	5	7	6	7	10	9	9	9	8	10	10
	SA	14	19	19	20	19	20	21	18	19	15	16	18	18	18	17	18
	ES	5	5	5	6	5	6	6	8	6	7	9	9	8	10	6	8
	WS	13	9	9	9	7	8	8	8	9	8	9	10	9	7	8	7
	MT	3	4	4	5	5	5	4	5	4	6	5	6	5	7	8	6
	PC	14	13	13	11	12	14	12	13	12	12	12	13	10	12	12	13
# SURVEYED		806	803	793	820	830	837	889	827	867	909	875	846	849	825	843	877

SEX	RESP	'72	'73	'74	'75	'76	'77	'78	'80	'82	'83	'84	'85	'86	'87	'88	'89
M	NE	6%	5%	4%	4%	5%	4%	5%	3%	3%	5%	6%	7%	5%	6%	4%	5%
	MA	19	18	17	17	17	15	18	16	21	15	13	12	15	14	13	14
	EN	19	22	23	22	21	26	21	20	24	21	20	19	17	18	18	16
	WN	9	6	7	8	8	6	8	8	6	10	9	9	9	9	8	8
	SA	13	19	19	20	18	20	19	18	18	17	19	16	16	19	19	20
	ES	5	5	5	5	6	4	5	7	7	6	6	7	7	5	8	7
	WS	12	7	8	8	8	8	7	9	6	9	8	10	7	9	10	9
	MT	4	4	4	3	4	3	4	5	3	5	7	8	7	7	6	6
	PC	14	13	14	13	14	13	12	13	13	13	13	12	17	13	12	15
# SURVEYED		807	701	691	670	669	693	643	641	639	690	598	688	621	641	638	660

Q: The industry in which the respondent works. (In broad categories.)

Responses:
- AG = Agriculture, mining and construction
- MN = Manufacturing
- TR = Transportation, communication, and other public utilities
- WS = Wholesale
- RT = Retail trade
- FI = Finance, insurance and real estate; Business and repair service
- EN = Entertainment and recreation services, professional and related services
- PA = Public administration

SEX	RESP	'72	'73	'74	'75	'76	'77	'78	'80	'82	'83	'84	'85	'86	'87	'88	'89
F	AG	2%	1%	3%	3%	3%	2%	2%	3%	2%	3%	2%	3%	2%	3%	3%	2%
E	MN	20	22	23	21	25	24	24	21	19	19	21	15	19	16	16	18
M	TR	5	3	3	4	4	4	4	4	4	3	4	5	3	4	4	4
A	WS	3	2	2	2	2	1	2	3	3	2	2	3	2	2	2	2
L	RT	17	18	17	21	20	21	20	20	18	19	20	20	18	20	19	18
E	FI	21	21	17	17	15	16	19	15	20	17	21	21	19	20	19	19
	EN	29	29	29	28	28	28	25	28	31	32	27	29	31	29	31	31
	PA	4	3	7	4	4	5	5	7	3	6	5	5	7	6	6	5
# SURVEYED		653	673	675	698	698	736	768	713	776	808	792	778	754	757	772	796

SEX	RESP	'72	'73	'74	'75	'76	'77	'78	'80	'82	'83	'84	'85	'86	'87	'88	'89
M	AG	19%	19%	18%	18%	18%	22%	18%	19%	21%	19%	15%	20%	18%	20%	15%	16%
	MN	30	28	29	29	28	28	29	30	26	26	29	23	25	25	25	21
	TR	9	9	10	7	9	8	9	9	9	6	6	10	7	8	10	9
	WS	5	4	2	2	3	3	4	3	3	5	4	5	4	4	3	3
	RT	10	9	8	11	12	10	9	9	11	11	11	9	11	10	13	13
	FI	8	8	9	11	10	9	11	9	12	10	12	11	13	12	12	13
	EN	10	13	13	12	11	11	12	11	12	13	12	14	14	12	13	16
	PA	10	9	11	10	10	8	10	9	6	12	10	9	8	9	10	9
# SURVEYED		767	665	669	646	654	680	636	632	623	678	587	675	611	635	621	642

access their personal computers. Iowa is a good example of a place where women and men are more optimistic. Asked about their expectations in the year 2000. 44% of the Iowans felt their lives would be better and 44% thought that life would be pretty much the same. 71% expect that Iowa and the rest of the Midwest will become a popular, mellow haven for those stress-ridden urbanites on the East and West coasts.

Welcome to the Field of Dreams Condo Development.

Q: **Do you agree with the following statement? In spite of what some people say, the lot (situation/condition) of the average man is getting worse, not better.** NOTE: Question was not asked in 1972, 1975, 1978, 1979, 1981, 1983, 1986.

Responses: **AG = Agree**   **DS = Disagree**

SEX RESP	'73	'74	'76	'77	'80	'82	'84	'85	'87	'88	'89
F AG	59%	63%	63%	58%	71%	69%	60%	51%	67%	64%	64%
DS	41	37	37	42	29	31	40	49	33	36	36
# SURVEYED	777	762	801	793	804	821	848	799	800	541	556

SEX RESP	'73	'74	'76	'77	'80	'82	'84	'85	'87	'88	'89
M AG	51%	59%	57%	54%	66%	66%	53%	47%	60%	60%	54%
DS	49	41	43	46	34	34	47	53	40	40	46
# SURVEYED	686	674	646	670	631	610	590	668	633	388	433

☛ 1980 and 1982 showed the highest percentages for both men and women who agreed that the quality of life was declining. The triumph of the Reagan administration apparently took some time to take hold.

☛ Blacks are particularly dour about the state of the average man, with 85% who agree that the world is going to hell in a hand basket in 1989.

☛ Kings and queens of pessimism by age group? For the last three years of the survey, it's a dead heat between the 36 to 41s and the 48 to 53s, each averaging 65% who agree that life is getting worse. Most optimistic is the 30 to 35s, with a mere 55% expressing a dim view of humanity.

But the world's still rotten

JUMPING (OR AT LEAST SHUFFLING) WITH JOY

If misery loves company, then misery must have some lonely days. 90% of the female and male respondents indicated that they are at least "pretty" happy with their lives.

Giddier they're growing too: comparing the averages of the first three survey years with the last three, we find that 5% more men are either very happy or pretty happy (85 to 90%) and that women registered a 4% increase (86 to 90%) in glee. Women are the slightly happier sex, however, in 13 of the 16 survey years.

During the Reagan administration (1980-89), 2% more women (love that Ronnie) ranked themselves as very happy (33% female to 31% male).

Why do women hold the happiness edge? One explanation may be the freedom and opportunities created by the women's rights movement. More educational choices. More employment choices. More independence. More lifestyle alternatives. So maybe more women are happier because they just have more.

But that theory may be at odds with other parts of the General Social Survey, which indicate that women are struggling to balance traditional female roles such as wife and mother with newer options such as careers and financial independence. Choice (it's my life and I'll do what I want), even when it involves conflict, could be the key ingredient for that overall groovy feeling.

With nets in hand, men are capturing that elusive butter-fly of happiness in greater numbers as well. Why do the genders glow so? Has the women's movement made men happier campers? In 1990, Peter D. Hart Associates of Washington, D.C. interviewed 815 American men from age 18 through retirement on the impact of the women's move-ment on men, women, and children. 74% thought that the women's movement had made things better for women and 48% thought it had made things worse for children. 40% thought the women's movement had made no differ-ence in their own life, while 31% said it had become worse.

And if the women's movement has not made men any hap-pier, are men doing their share to make more women hap-pier? We think not. A 1989 survey of 3,000 women across the U.S.A. found that respondents increasingly believe most men are mean, manipulative, oversexed, self-cen-tered, and lazy. And those were their good points.

So, apparently it is not entirely what we do for each other.

Perhaps the single biggest source of happiness for men is...the remote control?

And what makes women happy? The proliferation of mail-order catalogs. Maintenance-free hair (no construction zones). Call waiting.

And men asking what makes them happy.

Q: **Taken all together, how would you say things are these days—would you say that you are very happy, pretty happy, or not too happy?**

FAMILY ▼ LIFE

Responses: VH = Very happy   PH = Pretty happy   NH = Not too happy

SEX	RESP	'72	'73	'74	'75	'76	'77	'78	'80	'82	'83	'84	'85	'86	'87	'88	'89
F	VH	32%	38%	42%	34%	35%	37%	34%	36%	35%	31%	37%	28%	34%	32%	33%	33%
	PH	53	49	46	52	53	51	57	51	53	56	51	60	55	56	57	57
	NH	15	14	12	14	12	12	9	13	12	13	12	11	11	12	10	10
# SURVEYED		801	802	790	819	830	836	880	824	866	897	859	842	836	808	834	870

SEX	RESP	'72	'73	'74	'75	'76	'77	'78	'80	'82	'83	'84	'85	'86	'87	'88	'89
M	VH	29%	34%	34%	32%	33%	33%	35%	31%	31%	31%	32%	29%	30%	31%	36%	32%
	PH	53	54	52	56	54	56	55	55	56	56	54	60	58	57	56	59
	NH	18	12	14	12	13	11	10	14	14	13	15	11	11	13	8	9
# SURVEYED		805	698	690	666	669	691	637	638	639	676	586	688	613	629	632	656

☛ During the first three years of the survey, 15% of the male and 14% of the female respondents said they were not too happy. By the last three years of the survey, the depression had lifted for many, particularly men. Only 10% of the male and 11% of the female respondents said that life is a horrible experience relieved only by moments of boredom and alienation.

☛ Women reached a happiness "high" in the early '70s, as the women's movement picked up steam and the future, which is now, seemed ripe with possibilities. The scores correspond with female percentage highs during the same years in the "Happiness with Finances" survey.

☛ Grumpiest age group? 54-59, with a 14% not too happy response over the last three survey years.

☛ Do we get happier as we get older? We do if we're part of a survey! The very happiest age groups for the last three years of the survey are the 60-65 (36% very happy) and the 66+ (37%).

☛ Black respondents were a lot less happy: 21% were not too happy during the last three years of the survey.

No, I'm in a rut and I can't get up

LEAD AN EXCITING LIFE?

"I'm the chairman of the bored." Iggy Pop

The GSS reveals that: many women are bored. Or at least yawning. From 1987 to 1989, 58% of the female respondents said life is a muffled experience. This is actually an improvement over 1973-76, when 59% of the women polled said life is less than compelling. Television is no worse than it was 15 years ago, and we're watching it more than ever (45 hours and 34 minutes per week, prime time). So how come women find life so tedious?

We don't know. But while women kill the endless dreary hours of life waiting for something, anything of interest to happen, wouldn't you know that the majority of men are thrilled with their lives, climbing mountains, watching sports on TV, racing fast automobiles, cutting the lawn, flipping burgers in fast-food chains, sucking down beers, bedding desirable females, going to prison, stuck in relationships they see no way out of, sweeping hallways, making loads of money, and delaying fixing the car so that they can pay off the Christmas bills before the back-to-school expenses hit. For the last three years of the survey, 49% of the male respondents said they find life exciting, compared to 42% of the females.

We propose a new category to the question: do you find life exhausting?

Though males and females differ significantly on how exciting they view their lives, very little change over time has occurred, especially for women. The percentage of women reporting that their lives are "exciting" changes by less than 1% from 1973-1976 to 1987-1989. With more choice and opportunities available for women, how come they're not more excited?

Nothing new ever happens around here.

Slightly more men (2%) have found an "exciting" life in recent survey years. Perhaps they're now shaving without cream or have taken up hang-gliding over active volcanoes; maybe they've invented a new method for plucking nose hairs. Hard to figure what the source of all that excitement is. And what of the women who are excited to be alive? What special things are they doing? Is it money is it work is it sex is it children is it friends is it travel is it all-day mascara?

Differences between the sexes in the quality of life response can be attributed partly to how men and women answer surveys (with men usually more positive in describing personal conditions). But considering the consistent and quite pronounced lower satisfaction levels for women, more may be at play here than just style: more women may see their lives as plain less rewarding.

Surprisingly, the previous question on happiness with life, which sounds much like this one, provoked a different set of responses. In the general happiness quiz, men and women do not differ a great deal over the years. But women are the more positive in that question, responding in particular to the "pretty happy" category. So what are women saying here? Well...

"My life's okay, considering the average Ethiopian life."
"It's a shame *thirtysomething* was canceled."
"Pretty happy SDWF wants out of routine life."
"I'm very happy, in a depressed sort of way."
"At least I don't have prostrate problems."
"I haven't had a PMS attack in three weeks."
"The best date I ever had was with Mel Gibson. I doubt that he's yet aware of it."
"Cellulite is just a myth; those are speed bumps."
"Have a nice day."
"Life goes on..."

In answer to whether people are basically concerned only with themselves (Q1), a majority (49%) of the male respondents did not hesitate to answer "yes, they are" during the last three years of the survey. A mere 44% of the female respondents agreed. But that 44% represented a 4% jump from the first three survey years, while the male respondents showed no gain when comparing first and last periods.

The early survey years are also interesting in that men can't seem to make up their minds about the intentions of other people. For instance, in 1975, 52% claimed that other people were helpful, while 42% said they were not; the following year, 40% claimed folks were helpful, while 55% said they were not. What provoked such flip-flopping? Resident theorists believe it was a bad group experience at the muffler shop.

Men were a little more trusting on the fairness question (Q2), with a majority in every year answering that people would try to be fair (56% during the last three survey years, a drop of one point from the early period). But they still trailed women, who averaged 61% in the trusting mode during the same period. But women are losing their trust here, too. Comparing the first three years with the last three, female respondents who believe others would take advantage of them increased by 2% (32 to 34%), while the male response increased from 37 to 38%.

Q 1: **Would you say that most of the time people try to be helpful, or that mostly they are just looking out for themselves?** NOTE: Question was not asked in 1974, 1977, 1979, 1981, 1982, 1985.

Responses: HL = Try to be helpful   NH = Just look out for themselves;
DP = Depends (volunteer)

SEX	RESP	'72	'73	'75	'76	'78	'80	'83	'84	'86	'87	'88	'89
F	HL	54%	50%	60%	46%	65%	51%	60%	54%	59%	50%	52%	53%
	NH	41	47	33	47	30	45	35	42	35	46	44	41
	DP	5	4	7	7	5	4	4	4	6	5	5	5
# SURVEYED		793	800	815	827	883	821	902	871	842	819	554	589

SEX	RESP	'72	'73	'75	'76	'78	'80	'83	'84	'86	'87	'88	'89
M	HL	40%	44%	52%	40%	52%	46%	54%	49%	52%	45%	48%	46%
	NH	52	53	42	55	43	49	41	48	43	50	48	49
	DP	8	4	6	5	5	4	5	3	5	5	5	5
# SURVEYED		796	697	665	666	640	635	686	596	616	637	434	440

Q 2: **Do you think that most people would try to take advantage of you if they got a chance, or would they try to be fair?** NOTE: Question was not asked in 1974, 1977, 1979, 1981, 1982, 1985.

Responses: HL = Try to be helpful   NH = Just look out for themselves;
DP = Depends (volunteer)

SEX	RESP	'72	'73	'75	'76	'78	'80	'83	'84	'86	'87	'88	'89
F	AD	32%	35%	29%	33%	28%	33%	33%	33%	31%	37%	32%	34%
	FR	63	61	65	63	66	62	61	64	65	60	63	61
	DP	6	5	7	4	6	5	6	3	4	3	5	6
# SURVEYED		796	800	815	823	878	818	902	872	843	809	549	589

SEX	RESP	'72	'73	'75	'76	'78	'80	'83	'84	'86	'87	'88	'89
M	AD	37%	41%	33%	40%	32%	38%	37%	37%	37%	38%	36%	40%
	FR	57	54	59	56	63	59	58	60	60	56	58	55
	DP	6	5	7	4	5	4	5	3	3	5	6	5
# SURVEYED		796	695	661	668	637 '	632	683	595	613	636	435	440

☛ Table 1: The average annual gender difference on the category of other people looking out for themselves was a sparkling 7.25%.

☛ Table 1: The 66+ proved they grew up during a different time, as they seem to be the most willing to give people a chance. Averaged for the last three years of the survey, 56% felt that most people try to be helpful, an increase of 4% from the first three years! In comparison, 61% of those fun-seeking, self-centered 18 to 23s thought that most people were only concerned with themselves.

☛ Table 1: History plays a role. Blacks were less trusting of others than whites, with 32% responding that people "try to be helpful," compared to 52% of white respondents (average for the last three survey years).

☛ Table 2: On an average annual basis, men were 5% more likely than women to feel that people would take advantage of them if given the chance. Actual differences ranged from 1 to 7%.

☛ Table 2: Don't trust anyone over 25. The 18-23s were the least trusting of others. Averaged over the last three years of the survey, 49% felt that others would take advantage of them. In comparison, 70% of the 66+ crowd felt that their fellows would try to be fair.

☛ Table 2: Don't trust anyone, period. Again, blacks were almost twice as leery of other's intentions as whites. Averaged for the last three survey years, 63% of black respondents felt others would take advantage of them if given the chance, compared to 32% of the white respondents.

"I could tell ya, but then I'd have to kill ya..."
TRUST (ME)

The previous two questions dealt with trust in an indirect way, so it appears that the time has come to stick the topic to the refrigerator door with a magnet. Men, when they consider human nature, have so far had the more dominant level of pessimism. Male respondents are more inclined to believe that people are self-centered and waiting to swipe the shirt off your back. Yet more male (43% during the last three survey years) than female respondents (40%) apparently feel that the average Joe Schmoe can be trusted.

This is what we don't know: is this male trust thing qualified by the popular but largely unexplored "insincere used car salesman theory," first developed by Mel the doughnut baker during a slow period at the Friday night bowling league? Mel claims that people will behave notoriously most of the time (acting only in self interest, subtly eyeing your shirt, checking the collar for size). You therefore trust them to behave in a manner devoid of trust. For instance, you know that the used car salesmen will try to cheat you if he can. He knows that you know. Therefore, you have developed a bond of trust, in which you both implicitly agree that he, the car salesmen, will attempt to cheat and you, the potential buyer, will strive to stop him. While Mel's logic is not always good, we nearly see his point.

For female respondents, caution was a priority. The majority (57% during the last three years) of women consistently responded that you can't be too careful when it comes to other people. This figure was up 2% from the first three survey years. 52% of the male respondents felt the same way, up from 49% over the first three survey years. The rift between the sexes seems to be slowly but steadily closing, with men in the trust column steadily migrating to the "you can't be too careful" land.

Q: **Generally speaking, would you say that most people could be trusted or that you can't be too careful in dealing with people?**
NOTE: Question was not asked in 1974, 1977, 1979, 1981, 1982, 1985. 1979, 1981, 1983, 1986.

Responses: 　 **TR = Most people can be trusted** 　 　 **TC = Can't be too careful;**
　 　 　 　 DP = Depends (volunteer)

SEX	RESP	'72	'73	'75	'76	'78	'80	'83	'84	'86	'87	'88	'89
F	TR	44%	44%	35%	44%	35%	45%	30%	47%	35%	42%	36%	41%
	TC	53	53	60	52	60	51	66	51	62	55	60	56
	DP	3	3	4	4	5	4	4	2	3	3	4	3
# SURVEYED		793	801	813	827	886	825	313	865	846	819	557	589

SEX	RESP	'72	'73	'75	'76	'78	'80	'83	'84	'86	'87	'88	'89
M	TR	48%	49%	45%	46%	44%	46%	41%	49%	41%	47%	42%	41%
	TC	48	49	51	51	52	50	54	47	57	48	53	54
	DP	4	3	4	3	4	4	5	4	2	5	5	5
# SURVEYED		804	698	665	668	642	636	487	596	620	640	433	441SEX

☛ The average annual male/female difference was 5%.

☛ When the averages from 1972-74 and 1987-89 are summed, compared, diced, and sliced, the stats indicate that women experienced only a slim 1% decrease in the "Most people can be trusted category." Men, on the other hand, registered a 4% decrease for the same category.

☛ Once again, the younger generations seem less trusting of others than older generations. In fact, 72% of those 18-23s believe that you can't be too careful, compared to 51% of the 66+.

☛ Black responses were consistent with other trust-based questions. More than 82% said you "can't be too careful," compared to 50% of white respondents.

What would you do if I sang out of tune?

IMPORTANCE OF FRIENDS

"How often are we to die before we go quite off this stage? In every friend we lose a part of ourselves, and the best part." Alexander Pope to Jonathan Swift

The view from 3,000 feet: Women and men view their friends differently. After carefully studying the table below and reading a lot of books on the topic, we have concluded that women are prone to enjoying a greater level of satisfaction with their friends. In the top category (I really, really, very much like my friends) women led annually by an average of 6%.

The General Social Survey results support the studies of Deborah Tannen, best-selling author of *You Just Don't Understand*. Tannen believes women place a greater importance on intimacy in friendships than do men, whose friendships tend to be grounded in competitive or social activity. Women may feel their friends know them better, freely discussing matters of the heart with them. Typically, men reserve intimacy for their romantic relationships, aggressively avoiding anything resembling heartfelt talk with the boys in the barroom or on the golf course.

What we found was that men apparently do value friendships rather highly, but are reluctant to assign top value to them. Women, on the other hand, are not so inhibited.

If the top category is compared for the last three years of the survey, women clearly place more of a premium on friendships, with 35% saying that they get "a very great deal" (something like a really big shew) of satisfaction, compared to the 27% of the males who responded in that category. The female edge starts to disappear when the first two categories are averaged, with females at 73% and males at 68%. The gap gets smaller still when the top three

But the very happy wife is harder to find

MARRIED AND HAPPY? JOIN THE CROWD

The good news is that, over the life of the General Social Survey, the percentage of women and men who are unhappy with their marriage is consistently small.

The bad news is that the survey indicates that both men and women don't find marriage to be as out-and-out blissful as they did 20 years ago.

And it is women who have wandered the furthest from the decided dominion of very happy to the more ambivalent land of pretty happy, which is still not bad when you consider the state of political affairs in India. During those early survey years, the average female response to "very happy" was 67%, while "pretty happy" elicited 30% (together, nearly the entire survey population). For the last three years, the very happy declined to 59% on average, as more women (36%) were beset with a "pretty happy" marriage.

Men, on the other hand, chart occasional peaks and valleys on their happiness map, but as a group they seem to like being married just fine. 70% were very, very happy during the first three survey years; 66% for the last three. Does marriage agree with men more? We know they live longer than their single brothers, perhaps because tormenting their wives is such good fun. And generally, when married people are asked whether they would marry the same person again, men are more likely to say yes. In a recent survey, 50% of the women queried said they would not marry the same person again, while 75% of the men said yes, she'd still be my gal.

Another 1990 survey of 815 American men from age 18 through retirement found that 63% (and 75% of the married men) chose marriage (above sex, money, fame, or career) as being most important in their lives. 88% of the sweethearts would marry their wives again, just as soon as they returned from the mall.

Reacting to this General Social Survey, sociologist Norval Glenn suggested in a recent issue of the *Journal of Marriage and the Family* that marriage has "diminished hedonistic consequences for those who participate in it." That means ice cream doesn't taste as good after you're married. Sociologist Andrew Greeley, who also analyzed this data, gives marriage higher marks, reporting that the ice cream is still fine, but says wedded bliss is becoming harder for young women to find.

Married men, Greeley told *Psychology Today,* are nearly as happy as ever. He finds that disenchantment is much more of a problem with young working wives who feel pressured by the conflicting demands of home and work responsibilities, a situation that is getting worse. But married women, remarks Greeley, "are still better off on the average in terms of happiness' than their sisters who have not married or who are separated or divorced and not remarried. These two groups seem to be the major losers, and their number, alas, is increasing." Greeley reported in his book, *Faithful Attraction,* on a 1989 Gallup poll of 657 adults in "intact marriages." Asked if they would marry the same person again, four out of five married people said "yes."

And what would husbands and wives change in each other if given the chance? Approximately 60% of the wives surveyed by *Esquire* magazine in 1990 would change either their husbands personal habits (23%), temper (21%), or salary (20%). 17% would change hubby's family. And the husbands would change the wives' self confidence (35%), sexual attitudes (31%), sexual performance (20%), and appearance (15%). 14% of the wives and 10% of the husbands said they would not change a thing about their spouses.

What to make of all this: Is the rift between the sexes growing? Does the stress of modern life threaten the bond of matrimony?

Are our expectations much too high? Do we have too many alternatives? Or is the institution of marriage simply going through a routine period of adjustment with men and women retooling their expectations as we hurdle toward the next century?

Q1: **If married, taking things all together, how would you describe your marriage? Would you say that your marriage is very happy, pretty happy, or not too happy?** NOTE: Question not asked in 1972, 1979, 1981.

Responses: VH = Very happy   PH = Pretty happy   NH = Not too happy

SEX	RESP	'73	'74	'75	'76	'77	'78	'80	'82	'83	'84	'85	'86	'87	'88	'89
F	VH	67%	69%	65%	65%	62%	65%	66%	66%	59%	66%	55%	65%	62%	59%	57%
	PH	30	27	32	32	33	32	31	29	37	31	42	32	35	35	39
	NH	3	5	4	3	5	3	3	5	4	3	3	4	3	5	4
# SURVEYED		565	548	517	520	506	508	462	441	498	468	433	438	420	410	435

SEX	RESP	'73	'74	'75	'76	'77	'78	'80	'82	'83	'84	'85	'86	'87	'88	'89
M	VH	69%	70%	71%	69%	69%	66%	70%	65%	66%	66%	58%	61%	69%	66%	64%
	PH	29	28	28	29	29	32	27	34	32	32	38	36	30	33	35
	NH	2	2	2	1	2	2	3	1	3	3	3	3	2	1	1
# SURVEYED		507	511	478	453	459	446	420	405	463	357	430	381	372	377	405

Q2: How old were you when you first married?

Responses: -15, 15-17, 18-20, 21-23, 24-26; 27-29, 30-32, 33-35, 36+

SEX	RESP	'72	'73	'74	'75	'76	'77	'78	'80	'82	'83	'84	'85	'86	'87	'88	'89
F	-15	2%	1%	1%	1%	2%	1%	1%	1%	1%	1%	0%	0%	1%	1%	1%	1%
	15-17	17	17	15	17	15	17	16	18	15	16	16	15	14	14	13	14
	18-20	40	39	40	39	39	36	41	42	40	36	42	42	37	38	40	38
	21-23	22	26	27	25	27	27	24	22	25	27	24	25	26	27	26	25
	24-26	10	10	10	10	10	9	10	10	11	12	9	10	13	12	11	11
	27-29	5	4	2	4	4	5	3	3	5	4	5	4	4	5	4	5
	30-32	2	1	1	2	2	3	1	2	1	2	1	2	2	1	2	3
	33-35	1	1	1	1	1	1	1	1	1	1	2	1	1	1	1	0
	36+	1	1	1	2	1	1	1	1	1	1	1	1	1	2	1	1
# SURVEYED		718	730	713	727	745	737	755	709	730	770	729	725	715	702	697	723

SEX	RESP	'72	'73	'74	'75	'76	'77	'78	'80	'82	'83	'84	'85	'86	'87	'88	'89
M	-15	0%	0%	0%	0%	0%	0%	0%	0%	0%	0%	0%	0%	0%	0%	0%	0%
	15-17	3	3	3	3	2	2	3	2	2	3	3	2	4	2	4	2
	18-20	21	19	22	21	17	22	23	22	23	24	19	22	25	22	27	23
	21-23	37	35	33	34	35	32	34	35	33	33	35	33	34	35	29	36
	24-26	19	21	20	20	24	22	21	25	21	22	24	21	21	22	20	17
	27-29	11	10	9	10	12	12	9	8	10	10	9	12	10	10	12	12
	30-32	4	6	7	5	5	4	6	3	6	5	5	5	4	6	5	6
	33-35	3	2	3	2	3	3	2	2	2	2	2	2	1	1	1	1
	36+	4	3	3	3	2	4	2	2	3	2	4	2	2	2	2	2
# SURVEYED		677	580	585	543	544	562	533	506	502	554	447	535	482	473	474	499

☛ Table 1: Most middle of the road, kinda happy age groups during the last three survey years? The 30-35s, with 38% pretty happy, and the 48-53, with 37%.

☛ Table 1: Proving that the early years of a marriage are the most volatile, the least stable marital group is: The 18-23 (surprise!), with scores that veer up, down, and all around. For example, the 18-23s averaged 55% very happy in 1987, 75% in '88, and 55% again in `89. In 1987, 9% were not too happy, 6% reached that depressed condition in '88, and nobody was not to happy in 1989.

☞ Table 1: Over the last three years of the survey, black respondents are somewhat less happy with their marital state, averaging 7% not happy, 41% pretty happy, and 52% very happy.

☞ Table 2: A small but increasing number of women are marrying a little later in life, and fewer are marrying in their mid-teens. Comparing the first three years with the last three years, we find that the 21-23, 24-26, 27-29, and 30-32 age groups have all experienced a one point jump, while the 15-17 has lost two points.

☞ Table 2: Male marriage patterns have changed too: more are marrying earlier. Averaging the first three survey years against the last three, 3% more men are marrying in the 18-20 group and 2% fewer in both the 33-35 and 33-35 groups. Go figure.

No more divorce, Vegas style

TIGHTEN THE DIVORCE SCREWS?

"D-I-V-O-R-C-E," sang Tammy or Lynn a few years back, kicking off a spelling trend in country-western songs. Divorce, which some 20 or 30 years ago was something of a social stigma, particularly for women, is now much more acceptable. But that doesn't mean that the divorce process is any more enjoyable or equitable. When the nuclear family splits, it's often an intense molecular explosion with lifetime consequences.

While the male response tends to fluctuate from year to year on the issue of making divorces harder to obtain, more women (than men) are definitely saying yes to stricter divorce laws. While they call for stricter laws, women (and men) in increasing numbers are (reluctantly?) graduating to singlehood via divorce (see charts 2 and 3).

Although stricter laws may further complicate an already confusing state-by-state legal process, many women (and a lot of men) obviously feel changes are needed. Women (more than men) were especially supportive of increasing the difficulty of the divorce process, with a 12% jump in that category over the 16 years of the survey.

Women's dissatisfaction (and men's ambivalence) with current laws may be due in part to money. *The Almanac of the American People* fields the estimate that, in the year following divorce, a woman's standard of living drops by 73%, while a man's increases by 42%.

The call for stricter laws also may be a moral reaction to the "divorce revolution," which saw the divorce rate triple from the early 1960s to the early 80s. And it may be hedonistic: various polls show that married people of both sexes are happier than single people, even when they're miserable (that Zen thing). "My marriage is good," they say through clenched teeth.

What are the prospects of a happy marriage these days? A 1990 poll of 500 adults aged 18 to 24 conducted for *Time* revealed that 56% of the female and 55% of the male respondents feel that it is more difficult to have a good marriage today.

80% of the respondents feel that couples in their generation are more likely to get divorced than those in their parents' generation. And what about their parents?

Psychologists and sociologists say the divorce revolution is steadily reaching older Americans and longer-term marriages. Baby boomers have made divorce more acceptable, and their parents are picking up the habit. Although the divorce rate has been slowly declining since the early '80s, the number of divorced Americans 65 and older has increased since 1980 at a rate twice as fast as the population of older Americans as a whole. In 1988, that number rose to about 35,000. The U.S. now has 1.3 million divorced people 65 and older.

Q1: **Should divorce in this country be easier or more difficult to obtain than it is now?** NOTE: Question was not asked in 1972, 1973, 1979-1981, 1984, 1987.

Responses: **ES** = Easier   **MD** = More difficult   **SM** = Stay as is (volunteer)

SEX	RESP	'73	'74	'76	'77	'80	'82	'84	'85	'87	'88	'89
F	ES	30%	26%	27%	28%	25%	21%	23%	23%	26%	24%	26%
	MD	46	52	53	52	45	56	56	58	56	56	57
	SM	24	21	20	20	30	23	20	19	17	20	17
# SURVEYED		756	782	780	795	835	818	869	803	816	520	541

SEX	RESP	'73	'74	'76	'77	'80	'82	'84	'85	'87	'88	'89
M	ES	38%	34%	31%	34%	32%	28%	27%	26%	30%	28%	28%
	MD	43	44	52	50	41	51	53	52	50	45	50
	SM	19	21	17	16	26	22	20	22	20	27	22
# SURVEYED		648	636	636	656	611	601	655	662	592	409	402

Q 2: Are you currently married, widowed, divorced, separated or have you never been married?

Responses: **MR** = Married   **WD** = Widowed   **DV** = Divorced
             SP = Separated   **NM** = Never married

SEX	RESP	'72	'73	'74	'75	'76	'77	'78	'80	'82	'83	'84	'85	'86	'87	'88	'89
F	MR	67%	70%	70%	63%	63%	61%	58%	56%	51%	55%	54%	52%	52%	51%	49%	50%
	WD	14	12	12	15	16	15	15	16	17	15	15	15	17	17	17	15
	DV	5	5	6	6	7	8	10	10	12	12	13	13	11	13	14	14
	SP	3	4	3	4	4	4	3	4	4	4	3	5	5	4	4	5
	NM	11	9	10	11	10	12	14	14	16	15	15	14	15	14	16	17
# SURVEYED		806	803	793	820	830	837	888	827	867	909	875	846	849	825	843	877

SEX	RESP	'72	'73	'74	'75	'76	'77	'78	'80	'82	'83	'84	'85	'86	'87	'88	'89
M	MR	77%	73%	74%	72%	68%	67%	70%	66%	64%	67%	60%	63%	62%	59%	59%	62%
	WD	3	4	4	3	5	6	4	5	4	4	3	4	4	4	3	3
	DV	3	3	5	5	6	5	7	7	8	7	9	8	9	9	10	9
	SP	1	3	2	2	3	4	3	2	3	2	3	3	3	3	2	2
	NM	15	17	15	18	19	18	17	20	21	19	25	22	22	25	25	24
# SURVEYED		807	701	691	670	669	693	643	641	639	690	598	688	621	641	638	660

Q 3: **Have you ever been divorced or legally separated?** NOTE: Asked only if respondents were currently married or widowed.

Responses: Yes   No

SEX	RESP	'72	'73	'74	'75	'76	'77	'78	'80	'82	'83	'84	'85	'86	'87	'88	'89
F	YES	15%	13%	14%	14%	13%	15%	16%	17%	18%	15%	18%	20%	18%	19%	19%	17%
	NO	85	87	86	86	87	85	84	83	82	85	82	80	82	81	81	83
# SURVEYED		634	659	644	642	650	630	639	592	592	630	598	566	584	560	546	565

SEX	RESP	'72	'73	'74	'75	'76	'77	'78	'80	'82	'83	'84	'85	'86	'87	'88	'89
M	YES	14%	14%	14%	17%	14%	17%	16%	16%	18%	18%	16%	17%	20%	18%	20%	20%
	NO	86	86	86	83	86	83	84	84	82	82	84	83	80	82	80	80
# SURVEYED		627	534	537	501	483	496	469	449	431	493	378	460	408	402	397	430

☛ Table 1: Attitudes toward divorce laws have changed. In the first three survey years, men were, on average, 6% more in favor of easier divorce laws than women (34% to 28%). During the last three years of the survey, 5% fewer men chose easier divorces, lessening the opinion gap between the sexes to 4% (29% to 25%).

☛ Table 2: Although female respondents have steadily increased their support for stricter divorce laws, it has not come at the expense of the easier divorce law sector, but instead the "stay as is" block.

☛ Table 2: The General Social Survey shows that the 60-65 age group currently has almost three times the number of divorced people in the last three years of the survey than it did during the first three (11 to 4%). In spite of these increased numbers, the age group remains strictly opposed to easier divorce laws, with 66% saying "make them harder" (averaged over the last three years of the survey).

☛ Table 2: Black respondents were twice as likely to be in favor of easier divorce laws as white respondents, with an average of 50% saying "make them easier" over the last three years of the survey.

☛ Table 2: Age group most in favor of easier divorce laws? The 18-23, with 37% in favor (averaged over the last three years of the survey).

☛ Table 2: For the last three survey years, 60% of the male respondents reported they were married, while only 50% of the female respondents did. And 14% of the women queried were currently divorced, compared to 9% of the men.

☛ Table 2: The fastest growing category for men is "Never married," with a quarter of the male population remaining unmarried in 1989 as compared to 15% in 1972. The percentage of women never married is more slowly increasing, with 11% in 1972, versus 17% in 1989.

☛ Table 2: Far more women than men have lost a spouse to death. From 1987-1989, 17% of the females reported they were widowed, compared to 3% of the males. An unfortunate example of the life span gap.

☛ Table 3: It's not too surprising that both sexes have nearly equal numbers of people who have experienced divorce or legal separation. Still, death rates affect the balance. The average annual male/female difference is 1.5%, but neither sex shows more divorced members in significantly more years then the other. Compared to the early survey years, more people are now divorced. When the average of the first three years is compared with the average of the last three years we find that 5% *more* men are divorced and 4% *more* women have moved into the "Yes" category. One must keep in mind that this is a cumulative sample. That is, whether the respondent got divorced last year or in 1934, he/she will forever be in the "Yes" category. For instance, in 1981, 2.4 million people were married and 1.2 million divorced. Whence the infamous "one out of every two marriages fails" myth. However, a total of 50 million other marriages existed then, dropping the divorce rate for all marriages to 2%.

☛ Table 3: As older people from generations less tolerant of divorce die and the population in generations that readily accept divorce expands, the effect is a distortion that causes real change in current divorce rates to blur. The dying off of people from "low divorce" generations has as much influence as the population bulge in "high divorce" generations. Therefore very sophisticated statistical measures are necessary to sort out the current divorce rates. The question, "Were you divorced during the last 12 months?" might be more revealing of current practices.

Modern Family 101

WOMEN WORK, MEN SULK, CHILDREN IN TROUBLE?

During the 1980s, an average of 68% of the female respondents agreed or strongly agreed that a working mother could establish a relationship with her children every bit as wonderful as a house-bound mother. And what about the men? During the '80s, they manfully struggled with the notion of working moms, creeping to the level of support (55%) that women occupied in the '70s. On the question of whether men should work and women should stay home with the family, 47% of the male and 43% of the female respondents agreed during the 1980s, a precipitous drop from 69% (male) and 64% (female) recorded in 1977.

According to a recent survey, 94% of mothers who work outside the home said they need the money and 74% said they were tired all the time. (Even "Blondie" Bumstead, after 60 years of keeping house, has joined the workforce!) So they're not working for the sheer enjoyment of it. Out of necessity, women have to believe that they can make employment and parenthood mesh, since staying at home is no longer an option for many.

But what if it was? 79% of the mothers (and 39% of the fathers) surveyed by *The Los Angeles Times* in 1990 would quit their jobs, if they could, to stay at home and raise their children. 72% of the working mothers (1,000 households were surveyed) said they often worry about whether they're doing a good job as a parent. According to a 1990 *Time* survey of 505 adults aged 18 to 24, 66% of the female respondents said that they would, if they had the opportunity, stay home and raise the children.

A 1990 *Parents* magazine poll of 30,000 readers asked women if they would like to turn the clock back to the idealized world of the 1950s, when women stayed home and men went to work. 56% said no thanks, 25% responded yes, and 19% could not make up their minds. Another 1990 *Parents* survey asked working moms how they felt about at-home moms. 56% said they admire the at-homes, while 49% of the at-home mothers were critical of mothers who work.

Q1: **Please tell me whether you strongly agree, agree, disagree, or strongly disagree with this statement: a working mother can establish just as secure and warm a relationship with her children as a mother who does not work.** NOTE: Question not asked in 1972-1976, 1978-1984, 1987.

Responses: **SA = Strongly agree** **AG = Agree;**
           DS = Disagree   **SD = Strongly disagree**

SEX	RESP	'77	'85	'86	'88	'89
F	SA	21%	28%	27%	29%	28%
	AG	34	39	40	40	41
	DS	28	24	24	22	26
	SD	17	8	8	8	5
# SURVEYED		824	836	846	544	567

SEX	RESP	'77	'85	'86	'88	'89
M	SA	9%	13%	15%	17%	14%
	AG	33	40	41	38	45
	DS	40	34	37	35	32
	SD	18	13	7	10	9
# SURVEYED		681	682	614	433	423

Q2: **Please tell me whether you strongly agree, agree, disagree, or strongly disagree with this statement: it is much better for everyone involved if the man is the achiever outside the home and the woman takes care of the home and family.** NOTE: Question not asked in 1972-1976, 1978-1984, 1987.

SHE SAID ▼ HE SAID

SEX	RESP	'77	'85	'86	'88	'89
F	SA	18%	9%	11%	8%	9%
	AG	46	37	37	31	30
	DS	29	36	38	41	40
	SD	8	18	15	19	21
# SURVEYED		823	833	836	540	559

SEX	RESP	'77	'85	'86	'88	'89
M	SA	19%	11%	7%	11%	11%
	AG	50	40	41	35	32
	DS	27	41	43	41	46
	SD	4	8	9	13	11
# SURVEYED		680	669	608	424	418

☛ Table 1: The average annual male/female difference is 12%.

☛ Table 1: Although men are still on average 10% below women in the two "agree" categories, male attitudes about working mothers are undergoing change more rapidly than women's, with 17% more men responding in the two "agree" categories in 1989 than in 1977; the corresponding figure for women was 14%.

☛ Table 1: During the 1980s, the older the group (and the more distant from daily child care), the cooler it tended to be about working mothers: the 66+ block averaged 45% approval; the 48-53, 58%; 36-41, 73%; and the 24-29, 70%.

☛ Table 1: 52% of 1,100 pediatricians surveyed by the American Academy of Pediatrics and *Working Mother* magazine said children up to the age of three may be hurt by their mothers working full time. Female pediatricians and younger doctors tended to be less concerned about mothers working full time.

☛ Table 2: Support for the traditional "man work, woman keep house and family" model significantly eroded during the late '80s. In 1985-86, 50% of the males and 47% of the females agreed that this was the best way to go. By 1988-89, male support had declined to 45% and female to 39%.

☛ Table 2: Between the older and younger generations surveyed, a huge gap exists. For 1988-89, only 25% of the 18-23s agreed with the traditional arrangement. Within the 66+ block, 75% agreed that women should stay home and the men should work.

I'm wondering if it's fit for me

IS THE WORLD FIT FOR CHILDREN?

While a majority of the women (59%) and men (63%) surveyed say yes, the future will be a nice place for our children, the pessimists among us are numerous. From 1973-1980, the percentage of men and women who believed the world was becoming too unstable for a semi-responsible adult to bring children into it steadily increased, reaching an all-time high for both genders in 1980.

The pessimists of both genders almost became a majority that year, perhaps affected by the very lengthy and nationally demoralizing Iranian hostage crisis. It was a disturbing period in American history, as President Carter offered to trade large kitchen appliances to the Ayatollah Khomeini in exchange for future draft considerations, while Ted Koppel, bearing an uncanny resemblance to Alfred E. Newman, hosted the entire ordeal, becoming a media star in the process and giving away thousands in prizes.

Suddenly though, it was the Reagan years, and as violins played softly in the background, the world (or at least the U.S.) seemed to become a safer place in which our children could one day run amuck while assuming responsibility for our large credit card bills. In 1982, the optimists once again gained control, with 64% of the male and 65% of the females saying that the future looked good for their children. But for the life of the survey, 37% of the male and 41% of the female respondents stubbornly clung to the notion that it's hardly fair to bring a child into the world, regardless of whether it's run by Republicans or Democrats.

In all but two years, 1982 and 1985, women were more pessimistic about the state of the world in which their children would live. Two things comes to mind: 1) Obviously, they're harder to fool. 2) They have the babies.

The rather looping fluctuations from year to year indicate that both men and women's attitudes are subject to change, pushed by prevailing social conditions, personal fortune, stock market behavior, weather, prime-time television, and the latest national or world crisis.

Anyone else out there believe that the future holds less promise for our children?

A 1990 *Washington Post*/ABC News poll questioned 1,518 adults about national problems now and in the future. A majority of the respondents thought that it would be more difficult for young people in the year 2000 to find a good job, pay for college, buy a house, afford children, save money, or show a real interest in professional boxing. On the subjects of crime, poverty, pollution, inflation, drug abuse, and homelessness, a majority felt that these would be worse in ten years. Only in one area were they relatively optimistic: racial relations, with nearly 50% believing that the problem of racial prejudice would be better in ten years. More than 30% said bias would be about the same as it ever was.

Q: **Do you agree with the following statement? It's hardly fair to bring a child into the world with the way things look for the future.** NOTE: Question was not asked in 1972, 1975, 1978, 1979, 1981, 1983, 1986.

Responses: AG = Agree   DS = Disagree

SEX RESP	'73	'74	'76	'77	'80	'82	'84	'85	'87	'88	'89
F AG	40%	39%	45%	42%	49%	35%	41%	33%	44%	43%	40%
DS	60	61	55	58	51	65	59	67	56	57	60
# SURVEYED	784	774	798	806	802	817	855	814	797	563	571

SEX RESP	'73	'74	'76	'77	'80	'82	'84	'85	'87	'88	'89
M AG	34%	34%	40%	35%	47%	36%	39%	34%	35%	34%	36%
DS	66	66	60	65	53	64	61	66	65	66	64
# SURVEYED	684	670	644	675	626	617	593	672	626	388	434

☛ The average annual male/female difference is 5%.

☛ Those with the least power or experience may feel the most pessimistic. Consider that, for the last three years of the survey, 44% of the 18-23 age block agreed that the world is unfit for new kids.

☛ On second thought, it may be those with the most experience who are cynical. For the last three years of the survey, the 60+ crowd averaged 48% who agreed it was not fair to bring a child into world as we know it; the 54-59s, 44%.

☛ Or maybe it's the disadvantaged and the alienated? Averaged for the last three years of the survey, 57% of the black respondents agreed with the statement, peaking with a whopping 68% in 1989.

What would Madonna say?

SPANKING AS DISCIPLINE

For the life of this survey, an overwhelming 83% of the male and 78% of the female respondents agreed or strongly agreed that spanking is sometimes a necessary form of child discipline.

But spanking children seems to be losing some of its appeal. Over the four-year survey period, percentages decreased for men and women who agreed that a spanking was "sometimes" necessary, particularly among the gentler sex. In 1986, 83% of the female respondents said yes to spanking; by 1989, only(?) 74% held the same view. The male pro-spanking response declined from 85 to 82%, indicating that men are a lot less interested in losing one of their traditional methods of child discipline.

Q : **Do you strongly agree, agree, disagree, or strongly disagree that it is sometimes necessary to discipline a child with a good, hard spanking?** NOTE: Question not asked in 1972-1985.

Responses: **SA = Strongly agree**   **AG = Agree;**
DA = Disagree   **SD = Strongly disagree**

SEX	RESP	'86	'88	'89	SEX	RESP	'86	'88	'89
F	SA	29%	32%	29%	M	SA	26%	30%	35%
	AG	54	46	45		AG	59	53	47
	DA	15	16	20		DA	12	14	13
	SD	3	7	6		SD	3	4	4
# SURVEYED		847	545	570	# SURVEYED		613	433	424

☛ The average annual male/female difference was 5%.

☛ Consistent support for spanking exists throughout the age groups. Percentages of those 18-23 (79%) who support spanking were only slightly less than the 66+ (81%).

44

But I just wanna be like everyone else

INDEPENDENT THOUGHT AS A CHILDHOOD TRAIT

What quality would you rank as the most important for your children to learn? What characteristic would ensure survival in a complex world full of twists and quirks and quarks and bytes, not to mention working parents and Nintendized children? What trait would lend itself to delivering sound judgements on today and tomorrow's increasingly murky ethical dilemmas? What was the lesson that Thoreau and Emerson taught 150 years ago?

To think for oneself. American men and women most value self-reliance and independent thinking (of the five traits ranked in the survey). In every year, nearly 70% of the respondents ranked it first or second. More women (54%) than men (50%) ranked independent thinking first in every year. In all but one year (1989) the next largest percentage group of women ranked it second (18% to 17% for men). When the percentages of the two ranks are combined, women favoring independent thought have a 3% edge.

60 years ago, obedience to authority would have won out. According to University of Michigan sociologist Duane Alwin, a revolution in values has occurred. Alwin examined the goals of parents in the famous "Middletown" (Muncie, Indiana) research project, started in 1924, comparing them to a replicated study 54 years later in Muncie.

He found that mothers in 1924 Muncie ranked loyalty to the church, strict obedience, and good manners as the preferred traits for their children. "54 years later, a new generation of Muncie mothers had virtually opposite child-rearing goals," writes Anne Remley in *Psychology Today*. "Traits linked to autonomy, such as `independence' and `tolerance,' which received low marks from the 1924 mothers, were among these mothers top choices, while loyalty to

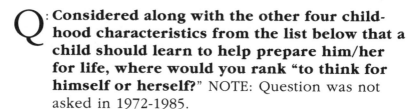
the church, strict obedience and good manners were selected by fewer than a fourth."

So how are the youth of today responding to this shift of emphasis? In late 1989, the Girl Scouts of America had a survey conducted which tested the moral views of 5,000 students. To the question, "If you're unsure, how do you decide what to do?" the respondents selected the following answers: do what was best for everyone involved (23%); follow the advice of authority (20%); do what would make them happy (18%); do what God or the Scriptures say is right (16%); do what would improve their own situation (10%); don't know (9%). 3% would follow their own conscience.

65% of the high school students surveyed said they would probably cheat on a test.

"To believe your own thought, to believe that what is true for you in your private heart is true for all men—that is genius." Emerson

"I hate quotations." Emerson

Q: **Considered along with the other four childhood characteristics from the list below that a child should learn to help prepare him/her for life, where would you rank "to think for himself or herself?"** NOTE: Question was not asked in 1972-1985.

  A. to obey
  B. to be well liked or popular.
  C. to think for himself or herself.
  D. to work hard.
  E. to help others when they need help.

FAMILY ▼ LIFE

Responses: 1 = First   2 = Second   3 = Third;
4 = Fourth   5 = Fifth

SEX	RESP	'86	'87	'88	'89	SEX	RESP	'86	'87	'88	'89
F	1	52%	56%	50%	56%	M	1	51%	54%	48%	48%
	2	18	18	18	17		2	17	16	18	20
	3	14	10	14	10		3	13	11	12	11
	4	10	10	12	13		4	13	11	14	13
	5	6	6	5	5		5	6	7	8	7
# SURVEYED		417	816	547	568	# SURVEYED		315	636	430	432

☛ Age group most supportive of independent thought (top two categories)? The 36-41, with an 80% average.

☛ Values from a different era: The 66+, with a 60% average, were the age group least supportive of independent thinking.

☛ 64% of black respondents ranked independent thought in the top two categories for the life of the survey. White respondents had a 72% average.

47

How to get ahead in life?

WORKING HARD AS A CHILDHOOD TRAIT

"Term, holidays, term, holidays, till we leave school, and then work, work, work till we die." C.S. Lewis

"Work expands so as to fill the time available for its completion." C. Northcote Parkinson

"Work is the curse of the drinking classes." Oscar Wilde

At some point in our short history, working hard became an American characteristic. During our frontier beginnings, no Motel Sixes existed, forcing men and women to take knife and fork in hand as they cleared land and built homes and waited for their neighborhoods to be wired for cable TV.

Today, working hard is still largely unavoidable for women and men laboring to keep from falling behind. However, despite the successes and sheer numbers of women in the workforce, the majority of men (35%) rated this trait as the second most important for their children to learn, while the majority of women (35%) placed it third. 32% of the females ranked it second.

Men may place more importance on hard work as a result of the traditional role of man as the dominant teacher of American business myth, part 1: put your teeth to the grindstone and someday you'll have one calloused set of gums. Women (a.k.a., nurturers) teach other worthwhile commandments, like helping others is good and you should always fold your clothes right after they come out of the dryer. But pushing theories of gender socialization and work habits aside, most parents want their kids to grow up as successful, financially independent adults; many believe that teaching them the virtues of hard work is one sure way to improve their kid's chances.

Q: **Considered along with the other four things from the list below that a child should learn to help prepare him/her for life, where would you rank "to work hard?"** NOTE: Question was not asked in 1972-1985.
   A. to obey
   B. to be well liked or popular.
   C. to think for himself or herself.
   D. to work hard.
   E. to help others when they need help.

Responses: 1 = First   2 = Second   3 = Third;
            4 = Fourth   5 = Fifth

SEX	RESP	'86	'87	'88	'89
F	1	9%	12%	14%	13%
	2	32	32	30	34
	3	34	35	34	36
	4	20	18	19	15
	5	6	3	3	2
# SURVEYED		417	816	547	568

SEX	RESP	'86	'87	'88	'89
M	1	14%	11%	15%	15%
	2	35	39	32	33
	3	31	31	32	32
	4	15	15	16	17
	5	5	4	5	3
# SURVEYED		315	636	430	432

☞ Although the gender difference is slight, it's also interesting to note that more men (14%) ranked working hard first than women (12%).

☞ 16% of black respondents ranked working hard number one, compared to 12% of the white.

☞ Age group that's the strongest advocate of working hard? The 18-23, with 18% rating it number one, 31% number two, and 36% number three.

☞ Age group that thought working hard was over-rated? 66+, with 31% ranking it in one of the bottom two positions. Rather go fishing, it seems.

Where can you get good Samaritan training?

HELPING OTHERS AS A CHILDHOOD TRAIT

While it's real important to Boy Scouts, helpfulness wasn't the most important trait that the majority of women and men in our survey would like to encourage in their children. And it should come as no surprise that women thought more highly of helping others. Although the gender difference was slight, more women (33% to 30%) ranked helpfulness second, while more men (33% to 30%) ranked it third. Of course, more men ranked it first as well (14% to 12%).

Men may balk slightly at ranking helpfulness more highly due to cultural conditioning. As boys, many men are taught that to get ahead, you have to work harder than the rest. And so they live to pass the message on to their children. The stereotypical and culturally acceptable "tough" male that yearns for competitive forays and the chance to prove what he's made of (sponge rubber? vulcanized steel?) may also lead men to rank hard work higher than helpfulness (although almost an identical number of both sexes ranked the traits number one). While not counter-productive to personal gain, helpfulness may not be viewed by the male, not even the altruistic Woodstock boomer leaning to post-yuppie values while listening to classic jams on the modern Walkman, as the best approach to "winning" and "increasing the net proceeds."

Women, on the other hand (Margaret Thatcher excepted), may value helpfulness more because 1) culturally, nurturing is encouraged and identified as a female trait; 2) they may well be more sympathetic and empathetic to the plight of others. Women may feel that they have less to lose and more to win by helping others.

Q : **Considered along with the other four things from the list below that a child should learn to help prepare him/her for life, where would you rank "to help others when they need help?"** NOTE: Question was not asked in 1972-1985.

   A. to obey
   B. to be well liked or popular.
   C. to think for himself or herself.
   D. to work hard.
   E. to help others when they need help.

Responses: 1 = First   2 = Second   3 = Third;
              4 = Fourth   5 = Fifth

SEX	RESP	'86	'87	'88	'89
F	1	12%	11%	12%	12%
	2	31	33	34	33
	3	33	35	28	32
	4	20	19	21	19
	5	4	3	4	4
# SURVEYED		417	816	558	568

SEX	RESP	'86	'87	'88	'89
M	1	16%	13%	14%	13%
	2	28	29	33	29
	3	34	36	29	34
	4	19	18	20	21
	5	4	5	4	3
# SURVEYED		315	636	436	432

☛ Women and men showed little difference (1-2%) in how they ranked helpfulness as an important childhood trait when the annual average differences for each response category are compared.

☛ Most altruistic age group? 30-35, with 50%, followed closely by 18-23 at 49% (combined average for categories 1 and 2).

☛ Least likely to rank helping others in top two categories? 60-65, with an average 37% in the top two categories, followed closely by 66+, at 39%.

Hey, Meet the Waltons!

MULTI-GENERATION HOUSEHOLDS

Households that stretch across generational lines are becoming more popular among men and women, particularly men. As boomers and their parents age, more and more Americans are waking up to a family reunion and, apparently, liking it. In 1989, 41% of women and 45% of men in our survey thought multi-generation households were a good idea, a huge shift from the early years of the survey.

Why has living with sons, daughters, parents, and grandparents become more popular? The high cost of living has imposed big changes on the "average" American household. Used to be that grandma and grandpa only came to visit, and that Junior's recent college graduation meant a clean financial break from mom and dad. But more and more people are reaping financial benefits by living under one roof.

And why are women more lukewarm about such a happy extended family scene? Women may feel the burden of additional household responsibilities that accompany extra members, since they remain the primary supervisors of domestic upkeep. It may be that women are more sensitive to issues of privacy. Good night, Mary Ellen.

And they make not like the in-laws as much. A recent *Esquire* poll asked men and women what they would change about their spouses. 17% of the female respondents said "his family."

And now we have a relatively new phenomenon: The "Grandparent Trap." Growing numbers of grandparents nationwide are becoming saddled with the burden of parenting their children's children, in what sociologists have dubbed **"Skip Generation"** families.

1990 U.S. Census Bureau show 3.1 million children living with their grandparents, a 50% increase over the last decade. Of those, nearly 1 million live in homes where a parent is not present.

Q: **As you know, many older people share a home with their grown children. Do you think this is generally a good idea or a bad idea?**
NOTE: Question was not asked in 1972, 1974, 1977, 1979, 1981, 1982, 1985.

Responses: GI = A good idea   BI = Bad idea   DP = Depends

SEX RESP	'73	'74	'76	'77	'80	'82	'84	'85	'87	'88	'89
F GI	30%	30%	34%	33%	39%	41%	47%	40%	47%	43%	41%
BI	58	55	51	50	44	42	38	47	38	42	42
DP	12	15	16	17	17	17	14	13	15	15	17
# SURVEYED	798	815	822	885	818	905	866	845	817	552	586

SEX RESP	'73	'74	'76	'77	'80	'82	'84	'85	'87	'88	'89
M GI	33%	32%	40%	37%	43%	46%	54%	41%	54%	46%	45%
BI	57	53	47	47	43	43	33	47	33	40	38
DP	10	15	13	16	14	11	12	11	13	14	17
# SURVEYED	697	665	663	641	631	688	593	615	635	436	437

☛ Economic necessity is perhaps the number one reason for the dramatic shift in each gender's acceptance of multi-generation households. From 1973-76, 55% of women and 52% of men were opposed to this type of living arrangement.

☛ Men lead women in the "good idea" category by an average annual difference of 4%.

☛ Percentages for both gender's disapproval have dropped significantly in 1987-89, with 41% of the female and 37% of the male respondents believing that multi-generation households are a "bad idea."

☛ Black respondents were significantly more in favor (58%) than white (40%).

☛ Forget about moving in with your grandparents. For age groups, the least enthusiastic about the idea was the 66+ group, with 23% who believe it is a good idea and 60% turning thumbs down (averaged over the last three years of the survey). The lack of support for the big family spread was also manifest in the 54 to 65 age group.

Our 7-Elevens are the best

HAPPY WITH YOUR HOMETOWN?

Are American communities on the rocks?

According to a 1990 *Time* poll, almost 70% of the respondents said life in New York City has deteriorated in the past five years.

The Greater Detroit Chamber of Commerce queried 650 area business leaders about Detroit's image. More than 80% thought that Detroit's image had a negative impact on the business climate of southeast Michigan.

Nationwide, survey after survey shows men and women's civic pride collapsing under increasing crime rates, poverty, and a growing sense of helplessness.

But—don't worry, be happy. Our survey results were somewhat more uplifting, with a majority of men and women reporting a high level of community satisfaction. In fact, they're happier than ever with their hometowns. Comparing the first three with the last three survey years, female respondents jumped a point to 67% in the top three categories. And men have pulled even with the women in the top categories of satisfaction, jumping from 63 to 67%.

DDB Needham's Life Style Study contacts 4,000 adults on a yearly basis, asking them some 1,000 questions, including "Would you be content to live in the same town for the rest of your life?"

In 1990, more than 73% answered, "yes." 40% were opposed to people chewing gum in public.

Obviously, an economic profile of our respondents would shed light on our optimistic results. However, women were 3% more likely to be extremely satisfied (top two categories) with their community. Interesting stat to note in light of women's perception of their increasing vulnerability to crime.

Q : **For each area of life I am going to name, tell me the choice that shows how much satisfaction you get from that area. The city or place you live in.** NOTE: Question not asked in 1972, 1979, 1981, 1985.

Responses: VG = A very great deal   GD = A great deal   QB = Quite a bit
            FA = A fair amount   SM = Some   LT = a little
            NO = None

SEX	RESP	'73	'74	'75	'76	'77	'78	'80	'82	'83	'84	'86	'87	'88	'89
F	VG	24%	21%	21%	20%	20%	18%	23%	17%	19%	21%	16%	20%	20%	19%
	GD	25	27	32	30	28	31	31	27	31	32	28	30	30	27
M	QB	17	18	13	18	17	17	16	20	17	17	19	17	20	19
	FA	21	22	19	20	21	19	18	22	20	18	21	21	21	20
	SM	6	6	6	7	5	7	5	7	6	5	7	7	5	6
	LT	4	4	6	3	5	5	4	5	5	5	7	4	3	6
	NO	3	1	3	2	3	3	2	2	2	2	2	2	2	3
# SURVEYED		802	792	816	827	836	884	823	864	902	866	843	819	558	586

SEX	RESP	'73	'74	'75	'76	'77	'78	'80	'82	'83	'84	'86	'87	'88	'89
M	VG	22%	19%	21%	19%	18%	15%	25%	14%	12%	18%	16%	18%	15%	15%
	GD	22	26	27	30	27	29	30	23	31	34	26	32	32	28
	QB	17	17	18	17	18	22	14	20	18	18	19	19	18	24
	FA	24	24	21	21	22	21	18	26	22	17	22	19	21	18
	SM	6	8	6	7	7	6	6	10	9	7	9	7	6	7
	LT	6	3	5	5	6	4	5	4	6	5	6	3	5	7
	NO	3	3	3	2	2	3	2	3	2	1	2	1	3	2
# SURVEYED		700	691	667	666	689	641	639	638	688	595	610	637	435	442

The survey shows slightly more men picking up the paper than women. But is the rift between the sexes more a variable of time or of interest level? One fact, which may shed some light on men's more avid newspaper reading, is that several widely read newspapers are linked to male-dominated professions, i.e. *The Wall Street Journal.* And then, of course, men have the sports' page to tantalize them.

Do women, to whom the majority of child-rearing and domestic responsibilities typically fall, have less time for or interest in reading a newspaper? Or is the gap deeper rooted in socialized gender differences? Is the difference disappearing as men and women become more acclimated to receiving all the news that's fit for television from the likes of Peter Jennings, Willard Scott, and Jay Leno?

Q: **How often do you read the newspaper—every day, a few times a week, once a week, less than once a week, or never?** NOTE: Question was not asked in 1973, 1974, 1976, 1979-1981, 1984.

Responses: **DA = Every day**   **FW = A few times a week**   **WK = Weekly;**
                LW = less than weekly   **NV = Never**

SEX RESP		'73	'74	'76	'77	'80	'82	'84	'85	'87	'88	'89
F	DA	65%	63%	63%	55%	52%	52%	52%	51%	52%	51%	49%
	FW	16	16	17	21	23	23	19	20	20	23	24
	WK	9	10	10	11	13	11	15	14	13	12	13
	LW	5	6	6	8	7	8	8	9	8	9	8
	NV	4	5	4	5	5	5	6	6	6	5	5
# SURVEYED		805	819	836	885	865	909	842	848	819	550	576
SEX RESP		'73	'74	'76	'77	'80	'82	'84	'85	'87	'88	'89
M	DA	72%	69%	62%	61%	56%	61%	54%	57%	58%	51%	51%
	FW	14	15	16	19	21	17	23	20	21	24	25
	WK	7	7	10	8	10	10	10	11	12	12	13
	LW	3	5	7	6	5	7	7	6	5	8	7
	NV	4	4	5	6	7	4	6	6	4	5	4
# SURVEYED		806	669	691	643	638	690	688	620	640	438	429

☞ 1977, was the only year that the percentage of women who read the newspaper every day (63%) exceeded that of men (62%). The gap in this category has ranged from a high of 9% to a low of 1%.

☞ Men were 4% more likely to read the paper at least three times a week.

☞ Which age group reads the paper the most? Daily readers are strongest in the 60+ block, although it also shows signs of a decline. Among the 60-65s, daily readership averaged 79% during the first three years of the survey and 73% during the last three. The 66+ group averaged 72% early, declining modestly to 70% late.

☞ Who reads the paper the least? The 18 to 23s, who in the last three years of the survey averaged 26% daily readers (down from 41% during the first three).

☞ Black respondents are reading less: an average of 39% read the paper daily during the last three years, compared to 52% in the first three. White respondents averaged 54% during 1987-89, down from 67%.

Not really, say women

SATISFIED WITH YOUR FINANCIAL SITUATION?

"My pleasure of thought is the pleasure of thinking
How pleasant it is to have money, heigh ho!
How pleasant it is to have money." Arthur Hugh Clough

When it comes to satisfaction with finances, the sexes have a different story to tell. Men are showing little change in their relationship with money, while women seem to be dealing with more financial insecurity.

During the first three years of the survey, slightly more women (32%) than men (31%) said they were "pretty well satisfied" with their finances. Since then, the satisfaction ratios have reversed, with male respondents (still 31% and holding) edging female respondents (30%).

This question is one of several that speak to either the declining or precarious financial status of women. Several factors are at work. Employment discrimination, the rising cost of living, more divorce, more single motherhood, and less education have introduced financial strains unknown to many women of previous generations. The wage gap, that now legendary 66 cents on the dollar ratio, continues to contribute to the delicate state of the female pocketbook. Of course, women generally live longer, so they can continue to earn less for longer periods.

"Up and down the City Road,
In and out the Eagle,
That's the way the money goes—
Pop goes the weasel!" W.R. Mandale

Age affects the level of satisfaction: the General Social Survey reveals a sizeable percent of discontented boomers. For the last three years, 31% of the 30-35, 27% of the 36-41, and 29% of the 42-47 age groups reported that they were not satisfied at all with their financial situation.

According to a 1990 Gallup Poll, aging baby boomers are increasingly pessimistic about their financial future and, consequently, are saving more than ever before. Of the 1,058 households queried, 62% of the general population and 75% of the boomers said they were going to save more because they feel that they will likely have to pay for a child's education, support an aging parent, and save for their own retirement at the same time. Social Insecurity may not be there for them either, but even if it is, it is likely to be a substandard financial safeguard (perhaps we've already reached that stage).

And what about taxes? Most men and women think that a new round of tax increases is on the way. A 1990 *Business Week* survey of 1,000 adults found that 82% felt that their taxes would increase.

A 1990 *Wall Street Journal*/NBC News Poll asked respondents if they would prefer to see a tax increase fall upon the wealthy or upon gasoline purchases. 68% thought about it for five seconds and responded, "The wealthy."

The *New York Times* recently asked 775 adults if they would be willing to raise taxes in order to reduce the Federal deficit. 87% thought it was a real good idea to increase taxes on people earning more than $100,000, while 85% would be willing to raise taxes on beer, wine, and liquor. The respondents were evenly divided on a general tax increase of $100 a year for everyone.

In late 1989, 814 Iowans, age 18 and up, were asked what one thing they would like to take with them when they die. Only 1% said money, proving perhaps that even if you could take it with you, you wouldn't take it with you. 9% said they would pack memories and 19% said they'd bring along the loved ones (supposing they don't want to go?). One respondent wanted to take a 12-pack of beer (hey, it's eternity, why not a case?) and another anticipated visiting the great beyond "with all my guns." The better to shoot those pesky wabbits.

Q : **We are interested in how people are getting along financially these days. So far as you and your family are concerned, would you say that you are pretty well satisfied with your financial situation, more or less satisfied, or not at all satisfied?**

Responses: PW = Pretty well satisfied   ML = More or less satisfied
NS = Not satisfied at all

SEX	RESP	'72	'73	'74	'75	'76	'77	'78	'80	'82	'83	'84	'85	'86	'87	'88	'89
F	PW	34%	31%	31%	30%	30%	34%	33%	28%	26%	28%	28%	28%	30%	29%	30%	30%
	ML	42	45	46	43	48	43	43	45	44	42	47	44	43	48	45	46
	NS	24	23	23	26	22	23	24	27	29	30	25	27	27	23	25	24
# SURVEYED		803	800	790	814	825	831	888	823	861	903	870	840	847	821	840	874

SEX	RESP	'72	'73	'74	'75	'76	'77	'78	'80	'82	'83	'84	'85	'86	'87	'88	'89
M	PW	31%	30%	32%	32%	31%	34%	35%	30%	26%	29%	29%	31%	31%	31%	31%	32%
	ML	47	46	45	42	44	44	41	44	48	41	43	44	43	47	45	42
	NS	21	24	23	27	25	22	23	27	26	30	28	25	26	22	23	26
# SURVEYED		805	701	688	665	667	690	641	639	637	689	594	685	619	640	634	658

☛ 60% of the respondents to a 1990 *Washington Post*/ABC News poll (1,500 surveyed) felt the national economy was getting worse. 43% believed that their local economy was deteriorating.

☛ "Pretty well satisfied" responses peaked at 34% for both sexes in 1977 and 1978, then dropped dramatically to 26% in 1982. By 1989, satisfaction had crept back up again to 31%.

☛ Overall, the differences between men and women are not great (1.4% average annual difference) over the history of the survey. Yet men show an increase in the "pretty well satisfied" response of under 1%, while the percentage of women in this category has dropped by 2%.

☛ Over the 16-year course of the survey, 25% of the population remained "not satisfied at all" with their finances (among minorities this figure was substantially higher, with black respondents averaging 41% and other minorities, 29%). Dissatisfaction reached an all-time high in 1982 and 1983, as a result of late '70s inflation and early '80s recession.

Ms. Average is on the skids

RATE YOUR RELATIVE FINANCIAL STATUS

Question: Where do men and women place themselves in comparison to Joseph and Mary Average, who on average (of course) own 1.43 cars, .93 modest bungalow in the suburbs, 1.67 cats, dogs, or birds, 2.31 television sets, .33 rotisserie grills, 1.1 blenders, and enough money in the bank to tide them over for approximately 2.73 weeks of unemployment?

Answer: Fewer of both sexes are inclined to call themselves financially "average," anymore, although for different reasons. And more than 25% of the respondents consider themselves "below average."

In 1972-74, 55% of the male and 60% of the female respondents ranked themselves as "average." During the last three years of the survey, those claiming possession of average financial empires had declined to 52% of the female and 49% of the male respondents. To where had the other 14% fled? Men tended to head for that special, sparsely populated place called "above average," but women increasingly described their financial travels as taking a turn down the bumpy road of "below average" or "far below average," where they frequently suffered "flats," or ran into "dead ends " and "road blocks," or sought aid at ramshackle service stations run by gap-toothed guys named "Dougie Boy."

Of the 8% of the female population that vacated the average category, 3% climbed to "above average" or "far above average." Unfortunately, a greater proportion (5%) descended to "below average" or "far below average."

Looking at the same figures for men, we see that 6% left the "average" category. But while slightly more than 2% downgraded themselves to lower categories, more than 3% upgraded themselves to above average categories. What's more, far more men (23%) than women (14%) had already considered themselves affluent during the first three years of the survey. Comparing the first and last three survey years, women have increased their share in the "below average" and "far below average" categories by 5% (26 to 31%). A significant contributing factor is the growing number of single mothers, who as a group have become America's poorest citizens.

Q : **Compared with American families in general, would you say your family income is far below average, below average, average, above average, or far above average?**

Responses: **FB = Far below average**   **BA = Below average**
AV = Average   **AA = Above average**
FA = Far above average

SEX	RESP	'72	'73	'74	'75	'76	'77	'78	'80	'82	'83	'84	'85	'86	'87	'88	'89
F	FB	4%	3%	5%	4%	4%	6%	5%	6%	5%	7%	5%	6%	6%	4%	6%	5%
	BA	24	19	22	25	24	24	23	26	29	25	23	26	26	27	25	25
	AV	60	62	57	55	60	54	58	53	51	49	56	53	51	52	52	52
	AA	11	14	15	15	11	15	13	14	14	17	14	15	15	17	16	17
	FA	1	1	1	1	0	1	1	1	1	2	1	1	2	1	1	1
# SURVEYED		796	797	787	814	820	827	883	817	851	894	866	837	841	817	833	869

SEX	RESP	'72	'73	'74	'75	'76	'77	'78	'80	'82	'83	'84	'85	'86	'87	'88	'89
M	FB	3%	4%	3%	5%	4%	4%	4%	4%	5%	5%	5%	6%	5%	6%	3%	4%
	BA	20	19	19	22	26	23	22	20	23	21	25	20	21	21	21	20
	AV	54	55	55	50	49	48	47	52	51	50	45	50	48	47	52	48
	AA	21	21	21	22	19	21	25	21	19	21	23	21	24	25	21	26
	FA	2	2	2	2	2	3	3	3	2	2	2	3	2	2	3	2
# SURVEYED		803	695	686	664	664	689	640	637	636	681	595	685	618	636	636	656

☛ Though not in as large numbers as women, men have increased their number in the poorest rankings, moving from 23% in the first three survey years to 25% in the last three.

☛ The most affluent age group in 1989? The 42-47 block, with 35% rating themselves above or far above average (161 surveyed).

☛ Poorest? The 60+ crowd, 33% of whom rated themselves below average (378 surveyed), and the 24-29 group, 32% of whom rated themselves below average (201 surveyed).

Climbing or falling off the ladder?

FINANCES IMPROVING? GETTING WORSE? WHAT?

The good news is that many people (men, to name a few) are actually managing to improve their finances over time. The bad news is that women don't share equally in this success. Comparing the first three with the last three survey years, female respondents actually suffered a 2% decline in the "getting better" category, falling from 40%. Men, those lucky economic creatures, increased by 3% their number who are "getting better," up from 43%.

Maybe time to invest in new golf clubs.

The best thing we can say about the economic condition of women is that they're maintaining the status quo more effectively. Over the last five years, the percentages for "stayed the same" stayed the same, ranging between 41 and 43%. Things aren't getting any better, but apparently they're not getting a whole lot worse: during the first and last three years of the survey, the same 20% of the female respondents said their financial situation was definitely declining. Stability is a beautiful thing to behold.

Better scratch that idea of buying an engine for the car.

What's holding women back financially? Divorce may set a woman back financially; a recent survey revealed that in the year following divorce, men improved their standard of living by 73%, while women watched theirs take a 42% dive. Motherhood may also inhibit the ability of women to compete for better jobs: a poll of 30,000 readers of *Parents* found that 50% of the female respondents thought they could compete equally with men, regardless of whether they had children. 40% said they could compete, but not with kids. If they could, 62% said they would work part-time and 25% said they would stay home.

Low-paying jobs are a great way to build character.

Unequal pay and a lack of opportunity (even in these enlightened times) are often factors that can hold women back from the financial trough, where men have been dunking their heads for decades (centuries?). A fax poll published by *Business Month* in 1990 asked readers to reflect upon women in the workplace. 64% of the respondents believe the number of women in upper management is "pitifully small." 55% believe that women still need laws to protect themselves in the workplace. 32% believe that discrimination is the main reason women haven't made it to the top of more corporations. 74% do not think that women have to act more like men to get ahead.

They just have to be paid more like men.

Q: **During the last few years, has your financial situation been getting better, worse, or has it stayed the same?**

Responses: **GB = Getting better**   **GW = Getting worse**   **SM = Stayed the same**

SEX	RESP	'72	'73	'74	'75	'76	'77	'78	'80	'82	'83	'84	'85	'86	'87	'88	'89
F	GB	38%	43%	39%	33%	34%	37%	38%	32%	28%	32%	37%	36%	36%	37%	37%	39%
	GW	19	17	23	30	24	23	19	28	31	29	22	22	23	20	21	19
	SM	43	40	39	38	42	40	43	41	40	39	41	42	41	43	42	42
# SURVEYED		791	781	788	812	826	830	884	823	864	894	869	841	843	822	836	872
SEX	RESP	'72	'73	'74	'75	'76	'77	'78	'80	'82	'83	'84	'85	'86	'87	'88	'89
M	GB	48%	41%	40%	38%	39%	40%	47%	38%	36%	39%	42%	42%	46%	44%	45%	48%
	GW	17	15	21	27	22	21	18	23	27	25	21	21	19	18	15	16
	SM	34	43	39	35	40	39	36	40	37	36	37	37	35	39	40	36
# SURVEYED		799	681	686	667	667	687	642	639	636	678	592	686	617	637	637	658

☛ Over the course of the study, an average of 38% of the total population said their financial situation has been "getting better." But men were more likely (by 8%) than women to respond positively.

And as more women accept employment, the traditional housewife is rapidly becoming an endangered species. By 1987-89, those keeping house full-time had dropped 25% from 1972-74, with only 28% of the female respondents fitting into this category. If the current attrition rate continues, we can expect the housewife to be extinct by the year 2008. And the year 2009...the era of the househusband, he of dominant domestic skills, begins?

Q: **Last week were you working full time, part-time, going to school, keeping house, or what?**

Responses: FT = Working full time   PT = Working part time   RT = Retired
UN =Unemployed, laid off, looking for work   SC = In school
TM = With a job, but not at work because   HK = Keeping
house of temporary illness, vacation, or strike

SEX	RESP	'72	'73	'74	'75	'76	'77	'78	'80	'82	'83	'84	'85	'86	'87	'88	'89
F	FT	25%	26%	27%	29%	27%	39%	31%	34%	37%	36%	39%	37%	34%	42%	39%	38%
	PT	10	13	10	12	10	9	13	11	13	12	13	13	12	13	14	12
	TM	2	1	2	1	1	2	2	2	2	2	2	3	3	1	2	3
	UN	1	1	2	1	2	1	1	2	2	3	1	1	1	1	1	0
	RT	6	4	3	5	7	5	7	6	7	7	8	11	11	11	12	13
	SC	2	3	2	3	2	2	3	3	2	2	3	3	3	4	4	3
	HK	54	53	52	48	51	43	43	43	37	38	34	32	36	28	27	30
# SURVEYED		793	798	789	815	828	828	870	815	848	891	871	838	839	813	832	864

SEX	RESP	'72	'73	'74	'75	'76	'77	'78	'80	'82	'83	'84	'85	'86	'87	'88	'89
M	FT	69%	65%	61%	59%	60%	67%	70%	66%	60%	62%	64%	63%	67%	68%	63%	67%
	PT	5	5	4	7	7	5	4	7	6	9	8	9	8	9	8	7
	TM	3	3	4	3	3	3	4	3	4	3	3	2	1	1	2	3
	UN	5	4	5	8	8	5	5	4	8	9	6	5	3	3	3	3
	RT	12	18	20	18	18	16	15	16	18	14	14	16	17	17	17	16
	SC	5	5	4	4	4	3	2	3	2	1	3	3	2	1	5	3
	HK	1	0	1	1	0	1	0	1	1	2	2	1	1	1	1	1
# SURVEYED		796	687	685	655	662	679	632	628	627	681	588	681	608	629	634	651

☛ Women show a significant increase in their retirement rate. A comparison of male retirees in 1972-1974 and 1987-1989 reveals no percentage increase, while the number of women retirees rose by 8%.

☛ Daddy tracking? An increasing number of men and women are now holding part-time jobs. And although the percentage of women working part-time is still greater than men (12% versus 7%), men are entering the part-time workforce slightly faster than women. Over 3% more men worked part-time in 1987-1989 than in 1972-1975, while women increased their numbers by only 2%.

☛ The age group least effected by the social change suggested in this question? The 60-65, with 29% of the females keeping house in 1972 and 29% still at it in 1989.

Responses: **SA = Strongly agree**   **AG = Agree**
DA = Disagree   **SD = Strongly disagree**

SEX	RESP	'84	'85	'87	'88	'89
F	SA	15%	7%	7%	4%	5%
	AG	45	31	30	25	24
	DA	32	42	44	46	46
	SD	7	20	18	25	25
# SURVEYED		812	814	836	536	559

SEX	RESP	'84	'85	'87	'88	'89
M	SA	12%	6%	5%	6%	6%
	AG	40	31	29	28	21
	DA	42	51	52	51	60
	SD	6	12	14	15	13
# SURVEYED		660	658	600	430	406

☞ The average annual male/female difference was 4%.

☞ Black respondents disagreed with the statement more so than whites: 79% to 72% in 1989.

☞ In the strongly disagree category, female respondents more strongly do: From 1985-89, women averaged 22% in the bottom category, while men strongly disagreed an average of 13.5%.

☞ Between 1988 and 1989, female opinion on this question stabilized, with very little change noted. Male responses were much more volatile, as the agree category sagged by 7%.

Hopping on the mommy (and daddy) track
IS YOUR JOB SATISFYING?

Men are a little less satisfied. Women are a little less satisfied as well. With their jobs. In 1972-74, 49% of the male respondents said they loved their jobs. Another 37% liked their jobs. In 1987-89, 47% really loved their jobs. And 38% sort of liked them.

More than 50% of 500 men polled recently by Robert Half International said they would be willing to cut their salaries as much as 25% to have more family or personal time. 45% said they would likely turn down a promotion if it meant spending less time with their families.

And women? In 1972-74, 49% loved their jobs as well. 38% said they were not in love, but they still liked their jobs. In 1987-89, 44% said they loved, really loved their jobs. And 40% were in the like phase.

The decline in female respondents' high-satisfaction response is probably related to a host of circumstances, including problems with childcare, level of employment, discrimination, stress, and other complexities, some no doubt created by the increasing number of women joining the workforce.

How are employers responding? A 1990 poll of human resource executives published in *The Wall Street Journal* found that 59% think that the availability of a flexible schedule will be a highly important recruitment feature in the future. Only 15% feel that it is important today. While 68% of the executives feel that the recruitment incentive of advancement opportunities is important today, only 48% believe it will be as important in the future.

A study of 521 firms by The Conference Board revealed that their personnel chiefs overwhelmingly endorse work options such as part-time employment, job-sharing, and flextime. 90% said part-timers and job-sharers are good workers; 80% said the same of flextimers.

Although the workplace appears to be going through a major transition from the old industrial model, it may be moving a bit too slowly for many women. But the situation could be worse.

They could be lawyers.

A 1990 survey by the American Bar Association, in which 2,289 lawyers participated, located a measly 33% who were very satisfied with their jobs. 55% of the women in solo practice and 42% in private practice said they were dissatisfied. 43% of the males in solo practice and 22% in private practice said they disliked what they do. The majority of lawyers surveyed reported that, as a group, they are: "less fulfilled, more fatigued, more stressed, more caught up in office politics, more likely to be in unhappy marriages, and more likely to drink excessively than they once did."

Sad, isn't it? But it could be worse. They *are* lawyers.

Q: **On the whole, how satisfied are you with the work you do—would you say you are very satisfied, moderately satisfied, a little dissatisfied, or very dissatisfied?**

Responses: VS = Very satisfied MS = Moderately satisfied
            LS = A little dissatisfied VD = Very dissatisfied

SEX	RESP	'72	'73	'74	'75	'76	'77	'78	'80	'82	'83	'84	'85	'86	'87	'88	'89
F	VS	50%	50%	47%	54%	51%	48%	51%	48%	47%	50%	48%	50%	47%	43%	44%	46%
	MS	37	40	38	32	35	39	36	34	38	37	34	37	40	39	41	40
	LS	11	7	10	10	9	10	8	14	9	8	12	9	9	13	11	10
	VD	2	3	5	4	5	2	5	4	6	5	6	4	3	5	4	4
# SURVEYED		315	625	713	716	730	728	756	737	734	769	727	692	674	654	664	683

SEX	RESP	'72	'73	'74	'75	'76	'77	'78	'80	'82	'83	'84	'85	'86	'87	'88	'89
M	VS	48%	49%	49%	55%	54%	47%	50%	46%	47%	48%	42%	45%	52%	46%	49%	47%
	MS	37	36	37	34	33	40	37	38	38	38	37	39	38	37	38	38
	LS	11	9	10	7	9	10	9	11	10	10	12	11	9	13	9	11
	VD	4	6	4	4	4	3	3	5	5	4	9	5	2	4	3	5
# SURVEYED		629	516	510	449	455	534	524	509	490	564	481	543	488	511	489	523

☛ Very satisfied responses fluctuated greatly over the course of the study. Men ranged from 55% in 1975 to 42% in 1984 (a 13% spread in nine years), while women's responses varied from 54% in 1975 to 43% in 1987 (an 11% spread in 12 years).

☛ Although the differences are not great, in comparing the averages of the study's first three years with the last three years there was a 3% drop in women's "very" and "moderately" satisfied categories, and a corresponding 3% rise in the "little dissatisfied" and "very dissatisfied" categories.

☛ The age group most likely to be frustrated on the job is the 24-29, with 16% a little dissatisfied and 5% very perturbed (you want me to do what?), averaged for the last three years of the survey.

Why are you asking me this question?

WOULD YOU CONTINUE WORKING IF SUDDENLY RICH?

Sounds just like Ed McMahon, doesn't it? According to a recent poll of 1,255 adults, almost 60% of the respondents said if they had a choice they would like to be rich. That was not surprising. 50% thought that you can be rich with an income less than $95,000 per year, while the other half believed that more than $95,000 sounded right. This was somewhat surprising: modern tycoon does not start at $95,000.

Anyway, the General Social Survey has a better twist on the get-rich quick question: If suddenly wealthy, would you keep working?

Believe it or not, almost 75% of the population claim they would keep working — even if they were given enough money to sail comfortably through old age and purchase that hazy trip to the great beyond in a class A coffin. But although they might continue to work, we suspect that they might adopt a new policy of blunt honesty with the boss. You talking to me?

Men, who tend to view work as a vital part of their self-esteem and identity, ranking right up there with attending sporting events and taking apart things they can't put back together again, were consistently more likely to say they would keep their jobs despite a financial windfall. Over the life of the survey, an average of 73% of male respondents said they would keep working, versus 65% of the female.

This response threw us. Maybe the question refers to a situation so fantastic that respondents couldn't quite relate properly: you have as much money as you'll ever need and you don't have to work anymore. But two worn-out segments of the population did understand, it seems, and they answered "yes, I quit" with no hesitation. Fully 50% of the 60-65 age group in 1989 said they would stop working on the spot and buy that condo in Florida. And according to a 1991 survey, the majority of working mothers (56%) said they would "consider giving up work indefinitely" if they no longer needed the money.

Q: **If you are working and you were to get enough money to live as comfortably as you like for the rest of your life, would you continue to work or would you stop working?** NOTE: Question not asked in 1972, 1975, 1978, 1979, 1981, 1983, 1986.

Responses: **CW = Continue to work** **SW = Stop working**

SEX RESP	'73	'74	'76	'77	'80	'82	'84	'85	'87	'88	'89
F CW	61%	58%	66%	63%	73%	71%	74%	68%	71%	68%	71%
SW	39	42	34	37	27	29	26	32	29	32	29
# SURVEYED	314	318	302	410	382	449	482	441	459	316	296
SEX RESP	'73	'74	'76	'77	'80	'82	'84	'85	'87	'88	'89
M CW	74%	69%	71%	75%	80%	75%	78%	70%	78%	74%	73%
SW	26	31	29	25	20	25	22	30	22	26	27
# SURVEYED	505	503	444	530	495	484	467	537	503	304	344

☛ An average of the 1973-76 responses shows that men were 10% more likely than women to say they would keep their jobs. In 1987-89, the gap had been sliced in half to 5%.

☛ In a 1990 poll published in *Parents,* respondents nationwide were asked what they would do if they one day woke up as millionaires. The most popular responses were: Give to church or charity (71%), buy a new car (56%), give to friends and relatives (51%), buy a new house or apartment (50%), and buy a new wardrobe (44%). 7% would hire servants, 8% would help reduce the U.S. deficit, and 28% would take a trip around the world. Most of the respondents agreed that $1 million is not enough to be really rich. Not with taxes and all those social events.

☛ 73% of black and white respondents agree on who would keep working: they would (averaged for the last three years).

level, people become more worried about finding a new job because fewer are available. During the recession of 1982-83, for instance, the number of people who said it would be "very easy" or "somewhat easy" to find a new job dropped 12% from the 1978 figure. 1982-83 was the only period that a majority or near majority of both sexes answered that it would be difficult to find another job with approximately the same level of status.

Women, who in the previous question exhibited more confidence about hanging on to their current jobs no matter what the economic climate, also displayed more confidence than men about finding a new job of equal value. Over the last three years of the survey, an astonishing 65% revealed it would be very or somewhat easy to locate a new job. Men displayed much bravado in the face of unemployment as well, with 60% answering that the job search would be "no sweat." However, male respondents were generally more concerned about their chances; for the last three years, 39% thought landing a new job would be hard work, compared to 35% of the female respondents.

Q: **About how easy would it be for you to find a job with another employer with approximately the same income and fringe benefits that you now have? Would you say very easy, somewhat easy, or not easy at all?** NOTE: Question was not asked in 1972-1976, 1979-1981, 1984, 1987.

Responses: VE = Very easy   SE = Somewhat easy   NE = Not easy at all

SEX	RESP	'77	'78	'82	'83	'85	'86	'88	'89
F	VE	26%	28%	22%	18%	26%	29%	26%	35%
	SE	32	32	27	33	33	34	40	30
	NE	42	40	51	49	41	37	34	35
# SURVEYED		401	386	427	435	431	397	296	291

SEX	RESP	'77	'78	'82	'83	'85	'86	'88	'89
F	VE	28%	29%	22%	20%	25%	26%	30%	33%
	SE	29	33	26	26	30	32	33	25
	NE	43	38	52	54	44	41	36	41
# SURVEYED		490	483	426	485	493	457	305	311

☛ The net result of the trend over time is an increase in the "very easy" response. When the average of the first three years is compared with the average of the last three years, we find that 3% more men and 5% more women chose "very easy."

☛ In 1989, 71% of the black respondents thought that finding a new job would be somewhat or very easy. 40% thought it would be very easy. However, respondents did not have this level of optimism during the other years of the survey, averaging 48% in the top two categories.

☛ Older folks tend to be less optimistic about finding another job of equal value. In 1989, 60% of the 48-53 age group, 55% of the 54-59, and 59% of the 60-65 said it wouldn't be easy at all to find a new job.

Employers' guide to dangling carrots

MOST DESIRED JOB CHARACTERISTICS

What are the ingredients of a great job? I'm glad you asked. It would be: 1) Great pay. (with bonuses). 2) Short work week (Wednesday mornings off for golf). 3) Corner office with a view (the lake would be nice). 4) Guaranteed job security (no way they fire me). 5) Work that was important to the future of the human race (like, grill chief or accounts manager?).

Not so, buffalo head. The next five questions ask men and women to rank five major job characteristics, providing a picture of the ideal work place. The most obvious variable, money, ranked surprisingly low among the choices.

Instead, Americans prefer to feel that they are getting things done when they go to work. "Accomplishment" was the decisive winner for both sexes. This intangible, subjective characteristic was the perk of choice for 70% of the population.

"Job Security" and "Length of Work Week" rank lowest on the quality of work totem pole, and seem to be growing less important. "Accomplishment" and "Promotion" are of slightly more concern to women, while "Good Pay," "Length of Work Week," and "Job Security" are of more importance to men.

So, to cultivate happy employees, forget the four-day work week and bragging about what a great place this is to retire from, and promote the heck out of that ineffable sense of accomplishment. And don't forget to throw a few bucks their way as well.

A good day is a productive day

LOVE THAT FEELING OF ACCOMPLISHMENT?

What makes a job special? The people? The money? The vacations? The knowledge that when you're sort of old and maybe kind of feeble, you won't have to do it anymore (if you're still alive)?

Both men and women declared that a sense of accomplishment is the most important thing. In particular, women appreciated work that was fulfilling. For the life of the survey, 52% of the female and 47% of the male respondents ranked doing a job well that was worth doing as their number one work objective.

Previously, we discovered that women, more than men, value hard work as a method for reaching that point in life called "success."   Now we find that women more appreciate a sense of accomplishment. What does this mean to the future of the economy and workforce? For America to remain number one in productivity, will the workplace adapt more feminine traits? Will men have to become more like women in their attitude toward work? Are women slowly but surely becoming the movers and shakers in the world? Are some foreign movies very hard to follow, even with subtitles?

In every survey year, more women than men ranked accomplishment in the top two response categories. But men are closing the gap: comparing the first and last three survey years, we find that 3% of the male respondents came to appreciate accomplishment more fondly (64% to 67%), while women stood steadfast at 72%. If women continue to remain constant in their devotion and the male appetite steadily increases, in the year 2525 men and women will reach the same level of appreciation for accomplishment. Mark it on your calendar now.

Notice the 8% dip for both sexes during the 1982 recession? With economic uncertainty clouding the job market, accomplishment became less important, replaced by concern over issues such as good (and regular) pay (in 1982, up 5% for men and 8% for women as a number one priority), job security (up 4% for both sexes), and food on the table (now very stale). Accomplishment appears to be best accomplished in an atmosphere of security, where more immediate needs have been met.

Q : **Consider the following job characteristics:**
1) high income,
2) no danger of being fired,
3) working hours are short, lots of free time,
4) chances for advancement,
5) work important and gives feeling of accomplishment. Among these five characteristics how would you rank "work important and gives feeling of accomplishment?" NOTE: Question was not asked in 1972, 1975, 1978, 1979, 1981, 1983, 1986.

Responses: HI = Highest NH = Next Highest MD = Middle
NL = Next lowest LO = Lowest

SEX	RESP	'73	'74	'76	'77	'80	'82	'84	'85	'87	'88	'89
F	HI	55%	56%	52%	50%	52%	46%	53%	49%	53%	49%	55%
	NH	17	19	18	20	19	16	19	20	20	22	1
	MD	13	10	13	13	14	18	13	16	14	12	15
	NL	9	9	12	11	10	12	9	10	8	10	9
	LO	7	6	6	7	4	8	6	5	6	6	4
# SURVEYED		783	779	799	811	801	320	853	824	807	561	550

SEX	RESP	'73	'74	'76	'77	'80	'82	'84	'85	'87	'88	'89
M	HI	48%	46%	48%	43%	51%	41%	48%	46%	47%	49%	52%
	NH	15	19	16	19	17	19	21	20	17	17	20
	MD	13	15	17	14	16	13	14	15	17	14	12
	NL	15	12	11	14	11	16	11	13	12	12	11
	LO	9	8	8	10	6	12	6	6	7	7	5
# SURVEYED		679	675	650	669	635	399	588	676	623	385	430

☛ The gender gap of 5% in the combined two highest response categories ("Highest" and "Next highest") was the largest of any of the "quality of work life" questions.

☛ What age group least valued accomplishment? The one with the least accomplishment, the 18-23, averaging 58% in the top two categories over the last three years of the survey.

☛ Meat and potatoes issues win out: black respondents placed accomplishment (48%) third on their list of job characteristics, behind good pay (65%) and promotion (55%). (410 questioned over the last three years of the survey.)

Second only to teaching those rabbits safe sex

WHAT ARE MY CHANCES FOR ADVANCEMENT?

How to become a big and powerful executive: In 1990, *The Atlanta Journal and Constitution* surveyed 200 Fortune 500 executives to uncover the top five attributes of a successful executive. They are: 1) Ability to communicate well. 2) Intelligence. 3) Integrity. 4) Experience. 5) Positive attitude.

Appears fairly simple: keep a clear head and learn how to talk and write good. Working our way to the top of the employment heap is one of the great American dreams; with a little bit of luck, anyone could do it, even your cousin Normie. Women remain slightly more ambitious (and harder working and more accomplishment oriented) than men. For the life of the survey, 58% of the male respondents ranked the potential for advancement in the top two positions, compared to 59% of the female respondents.

For the last three years, 19% of the female and 18% of the male respondents rated advancement potential as the number one job incentive, while 34% of the men and 37% of the women ranked it second. The average annual difference between the sexes was about 3%, with as many as 61% and as few as 48% of women ranking promotion in the top two response categories. In 1974, men actually exceeded women (59% male versus 54% female), but then Nixon resigned and that was the end of that. During two years of the survey ('77 and '82), the sexes did not differ in the upper two categories.

Women in the workforce are obviously ambitious, looking for ways to scale corporate ladders or surmount dangerous executive moats. So what does it take for women to advance in corporate cultures? In late 1990, *The Dallas Morning News* published results taken from the study

Moving Up...Moving On, conducted by Drs. Griffin and Connie Grant of Texas Women's University and Women's Center of Dallas and focusing on promotional requirements of women and their companies. It found that corporations and their women managers differ significantly in their perceptions of the minimal promotion requirements. While 55% of the managers thought additional communication skills were important, 83% of the companies concurred. 53% of the women identified additional interpersonal skills a requirement, while 81% of their companies did. A similar gap of 25% existed in the additional cognitive skills category. The managers and their companies were in agreement on one requirement: more than 70% agreed that additional leadership skills were needed. Other requirements that the companies rated more highly than the female managers included additional administrative skills and on-the-job training.

With apologies to John Molloy, how do women dress for success? The results of a 1990 poll of employed women across the nation presented the profile "of a working woman who is just as apt to wear casual sportswear to work as she is a tailored suit." The survey, appearing in *Apparel Merchandising,* found that the majority were more likely to buy and wear pants (51%) than dresses (41%). 28% said it was very likely that they would wear suits to work. 62% usually shop for a special piece of clothing to wear with an item that they already own, rather than shopping for a complete outfit. More than 50% prefer clothes that can be worn to work and on weekends. 55% of the men surveyed by the monthly *Shorts Illustrated* said they prefer going to the workplace in bermudas, weather permitting.

Assuming they're wearing the right type of clothing, how is corporate life treating women at the top? In 1990, *Business Week* published a survey of 450 female executives at corporations with at least $100 million in annual sales or at least 1,500 employees. 49% thought it would be longer than 10 years before their company would name a woman as CEO. While 63% think that large corporations are "pretty good" places for women executives to work, 60% thought that "a male-dominated corporate culture" was an obstacle to success for the women executives.

And what's life like at the bottom? A recent survey of more than 300 college graduates, published in *The Atlanta Journal and Constitution,* found that 69% of the respondents expected to spend two years or less in an entry level position before receiving a promotion. 24% expected to pay their dues for less than one year.

Apparently, patience is not being taught at the college level.

Q: **Consider the following job characteristics:**
1) high income,
2) no danger of being fired,
3) working hours are short, lot's of free time,
4) chances for advancement,
5) work important and gives a feeling of accomplishment. Among these five characteristics how would you rank "chances for advancement"? NOTE: Question was not asked in 1972, 1975, 1978, 1979, 1981, 1983, 1986.

MONEY ▼ JOBS

SEX	RESP	'73	'74	'76	'77	'80	'82	'84	'85	'87	'88	'89
F	HI	17%	16%	18%	18%	20%	14%	18%	23%	18%	21%	18%
	NH	39	38	39	36	36	34	38	38	38	34	38
	MD	23	25	21	24	25	20	23	23	21	24	27
	NL	12	13	14	13	12	21	13	11	15	14	12
	LO	10	8	8	9	6	11	7	4	7	7	6
# SURVEYED		783	779	799	811	801	320	853	824	807	561	550

SEX	RESP	'73	'74	'76	'77	'80	'82	'84	'85	'87	'88	'89
M	HI	19%	21%	17%	22%	18%	20%	21%	22%	18%	19%	17%
	NH	32	38	34	32	33	28	33	34	32	35	36
	MD	24	20	21	22	26	22	24	22	27	22	23
	NL	15	13	16	15	15	22	14	15	16	14	17
	LO	10	8	11	8	9	9	8	7	8	11	8
# SURVEYED		679	675	650	669	635	399	588	676	623	385	430

☛ When the average of the first three years is compared with the average of the last three years, we find that slightly more than 1% of the male respondents chose either "highest" or "next highest" in the early survey years (54% in 1973-76, 52% in 1987-89). Women showed no corresponding decrease in the top categories, registering 56% during both periods.

☛ During the recession both men and women lowered their high regard (and possibly their expectations) for promotion. In 1982, only 42% of males and females ranked promotion highly.

☛ Which age group valued advancement most highly? Oddly enough, it was the 66+ block, with scores significantly above the average. For the last three years of the survey, more than 63% rated promotion in the top two categories (586 surveyed).

☛ The age group least concerned with promotion? The 30-35, with 49% ranking it in the top two categories (70% of this age group ranked accomplishment in the top two categories).

Money, that's what I want?

HIGH PAY AS A JOB INCENTIVE

All along, we thought it was money that we wanted. Off we'd go, whistling to work, ready for the thrill of oiling our palms with some greasy bread. You know, dough. Greenbacks. Legal tender. Currency. Capital. Liquid assets. The almighty dollar. Wampum. Simoleons. Bucks. Filthy lucre. Hard cash. Dinero. Sawbucks. Fins. C-notes. G-notes. Smackers. Ah, let me count the ways I can say moolah. It's money that matters, we assumed. But we were wrong.

Money came in third, behind accomplishment and advancement. Money, of course, has its big fans among both men and women and may yet give advancement a strong run for the...money in the annual job characteristics sweepstakes. For the life of the survey, more men actually ranked money in the top spot (21%) than promotion (19%). 17% of the female respondents ranked advancement number one, while 21% thought money was the best thing about work.

Although the concern with income is shared on a relatively equal basis among both sexes, men are more bottom-line oriented. For the life of the survey, 47% of the male respondents ranked wages in the top two positions, compared to 44% of the female respondents. In all but one survey year more male than female respondents ranked income higher. However, if current trends continue, women may soon become more wage-centered than men as they go after their 66 cents on the dollar. From 1973-1976 to 1987-1989 (three-year averages) the number of women ranking wages in the top two categories rose from 40 to 45%. In the same time period, men increased their basic appetite for long green from 43 to 46%.

Of the five quality of work life questions, concern for wages is the most single most volatile, dropping off in good economic periods and roaring back during bad. Not surprisingly, income rose to its highest point during the recession in 1982. Females gave money a 28% rating in the number one category, a good 3% above the male rating and 6% more than any other charted year for women. The 25% in the top spot that men gave money was likewise a peak for them, matched only by their total for 1987. And speaking of 1987, men showed a high degree of concern that year, with 54% ranking income in the top two categories. What happened in 1987? You may recall October 19, otherwise known as Black Monday, the day the Dow stock market average plunged 508 points. The horror. Women, however, seemed much less involved in the whole stock market collapse atmosphere, with only 45% registering in the top categories. As one woman put it: why concern yourself with the gravy when you're still looking for the biscuit?

While money earned a relatively high ranking among both sexes in 1989, we expect that the 1990 and 1991 surveys will show even more of an increase due to the recession. A number of economic factors are squeezing workers: Many of the more than 21 million Americans who work part time will likely be affected by the economic downturn. A number of states facing fiscal crises are balancing their budgets in part by cutting safety-net programs for the people at poverty level, estimated to be some 32 million nationwide. And the service sector, one of the largest employers of women, has been severely hit by the recession. Consider retail: During the first 10 months of this recession, which began in July 1990, 398,000 retail jobs disappeared, accounting for 25% of the 1.5 million people who lost their jobs in that period. For the first 10 months of the downturn in 1981-82, retail employment fell by 23,000.

And we thought we had problems then.

More semi-depressing news: Americans' standard of living declined slightly in 1990, a situation that had not occurred since 1982. Among the seven richest industrialized nations, the U.S. was the only nation to suffer an outright drop in living standards last year.

So look for money to make a strong run at advancement for the number two position in 1990-91. And accomplishment shouldn't feel too secure, either.

Q : **Consider the following job characteristics: 1) high income, 2) no danger of being fired, 3) working hours are short, lots of free time, 4) chances for advancement, 5) work important and gives a feeling of accomplishment. Among these five characteristics how would you rank "high income?"** NOTE: Question was not asked in 1972, 1975, 1978, 1979, 1981, 1983, 1986.

Responses: HI = Highest   NH = Next Highest   MD = Middle
NL = Next lowest   LO = Lowest

SEX	RESP	'73	'74	'76	'77	'80	'82	'84	'85	'87	'88	'89
F	HI	19%	19%	19%	21%	20%	28%	18%	20%	20%	22%	20%
	NH	22	21	21	22	25	22	24	24	25	23	26
	MD	33	32	34	32	33	24	33	29	32	31	29
	NL	20	20	21	19	17	20	20	22	16	19	21
	LO	7	8	5	6	5	5	4	6	6	6	4
# SURVEYED		783	779	799	811	801	320	853	824	807	561	550

SEX	RESP	'73	'74	'76	'77	'80	'82	'84	'85	'87	'88	'89
M	HI	19%	18%	22%	20%	20%	25%	20%	19%	25%	20%	23%
	NH	26	20	25	27	28	28	26	28	29	26	24
	MD	29	30	31	29	32	28	32	33	29	36	36
	NL	19	21	18	16	15	14	18	17	13	14	13
	LO	8	10	5	7	5	5	4	2	5	3	3
# SURVEYED		679	675	650	669	635	399	588	676	623	385	430

☛ The younger (and less financially stable) the age group, the more highly it ranks wages. For instance, 60% of the 18-23, 46% of the 42-47, and 37% of the 60-65 age blocks rank income in the top two categories (over the last three survey years).

☛ Income is the number one concern of black respondents, with 65% (averaged for the last three years of the survey) ranking it in the top two spots, a 4% increase from the first three years of the survey. For the last three survey years, 44% of the white respondents placed wages in the top categories, likewise a 4% jump from 1973-76.

Above unemployment and below everything else

HOW DO YOU RATE JOB SECURITY?

The concern over job security ain't what it used to be. Tenure ranks significantly ahead of length of work week and significantly behind wages. The importance of job security is declining, as more workers with Great Depression era memories and anxieties leave the workforce and are replaced by twentysomethings and boomers, many of whom have never known job security except as part of history classes. A generation whose acceptable vision of reality is: white water rafting sans oars while headed toward the falls, suitcase in hand. Even unions, those bastions of job security protection, are on the decrease; union member-ship has dropped 15% in the last 10 years to 17 million in 1989. Meanwhile, union representation of the workforce decreased from 25 to 17%.

In every survey year, security was more important to men than women, although the male concern is declining more dramatically. For the life of the survey, 22% of the male and 19% of the female respondents ranked job security in one of the top two categories. In those categories, the average annual gender gap is about 4%. This difference is fairly consistent, dropping during recessionary periods (1976, 1982, and 1984) to 1-2%.

Women may see job security as slightly less of an issue due to the flexibility they require during the childcare years, when they may leave and then rejoin the workforce. In two-income households, they are also less likely to be the main wage-earner; men on average still earn nearly a third more than women.

Perhaps few expect security in this day of mergers, acqui-sitions, lay-offs, and job mobility. And maybe job securi-ty was a singular evanescent phenomenon of late industrialized America, bowing in during the halcyon flush of the post WWII baby boom bingo. Housing was cheap, companies expanded like gangbusters, and the country was on the move, economically staking out territory in Europe, Africa, the Third World, and California. But that was then and this is now: the '80s was the era of winner take all, as gold-rush fever and federal apathy led to a frantic wave of acquisition and merger mania that apparently did for job security what Michael Milken and Charles Keating did to the S&L industry. A 1990 poll in *The Atlantic Journal and Constitution* revealed that only 4% of the respondents believed that employees came out on top after a merger. 50% thought that executives benefitted the most; 35% thought the stockholders prospered. A 1990 *Time* poll reported that 62% of the respondents thought mergers and takeovers hurt employees; 80% thought it was the lawyers and bankers who most benefitted.

The other side of the coin: we don't expect job security because we don't want it anymore. *Business Week* notes that boomer job loyalties are weakening, as boomers continue to travel through life more faithful to intuition and instinct than societal expectations, often switching jobs and even careers. Facing permanent job insecurity and a higher level of turbulence becomes a way of life. Among the 30-35, 36-41, and 42-47 age groups, 5% of the respondents ranked security in the top spot, while 10% ranked it second. 67% ranked job security in one of the two bottom categories.

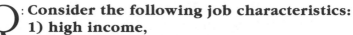
Q: Consider the following job characteristics:
1) high income,
2) no danger of being fired,
3) working hours are short, lots of free time,
4) chances for advancement,
5) work important and gives a feeling of accomplishment. Among these five characteristics how would you rank "no danger of being fired?" NOTE: Question was not asked in 1972, 1975, 1978, 1979, 1981, 1983, 1986.

Responses: HI = Highest   NH = Next Highest   MD = Middle
            NL = Next lowest   LO = Lowest

SEX	RESP	'73	'74	'76	'77	'80	'82	'84	'85	'87	'88	'89
F	HI	5%	5%	7%	6%	5%	9%	7%	6%	6%	6%	5%
	NH	12	10	15	14	11	18	13	11	9	13	11
	MD	19	21	21	22	18	24	21	22	22	23	23
	NL	34	32	31	33	34	27	35	37	35	30	35
	LO	29	32	27	25	32	22	24	23	29	28	26
# SURVEYED		783	779	799	811	801	320	853	824	807	561	550

SEX	RESP	'73	'74	'76	'77	'80	'82	'84	'85	'87	'88	'89
M	HI	8%	10%	9%	10%	7%	11%	8%	9%	6%	8%	6%
	NH	17	12	15	14	13	17	14	11	14	15	13
	MD	21	19	19	22	16	22	19	18	18	16	18
	NL	25	25	32	30	33	30	36	33	32	34	34
	LO	29	35	25	24	31	20	23	29	30	27	29
# SURVEYED		679	675	650	669	635	399	588	676	623	385	430

☛ Both males and females lowered their concern for job security over the last two decades. In the first three survey years, 24% of the male and 18% of the female respondents ranked job security in the top two categories. During the last three years, males averaged 21% and females 17%.

☛ Those nearing retirement age — but still far enough away to experience anxiety about getting there — were apt to rate security more highly: In 1988 and 1989, 25% of the 48-53 age group rated security in the top two categories.

☛ Concern with job security related to difficulty or ease in locating employment? Black and other minority respondents valued job security more than white respondents did: For the last three years of the survey, 26% of the minority respondents placed job security in the top two categories, compared to 15% of the white respondents.

The winners of the rat race may be the rats

IS LOTS OF FREE TIME IMPORTANT?

Although the length of the American work week has been declining for most of this century (at least on paper), during the '80s the hours started shifting the other way. The average work week for a full-time American worker increased from 42.5 hours in 1980 to 43.5 hours in 1990, according to the Bureau of Labor Statistics. And according to the General Social Survey, most men and women aren't particularly attracted to jobs with short working hours. In fact, of the five job characteristics listed, a diminutive work week with a corresponding increase in leisure hours has been ranked dead last in every survey since 1973.

In fact, it seems to be downright American to sneer at the suggestion of shorter work weeks: among age groups, the shorter week always was ranked last, with no discernable difference between the group rankings; white, black, and other minority respondents all ranked it basically the same; and men and women were in full agreement. No one seems to care much about shortening the work week!   We want accomplishment! Advancement! Money! Sometimes job security! But we like working hard for that stuff.

To further prove the point that men and women are not much concerned with shortening the common work week, question 2 asks them to indicate how many hours they worked during the previous week. On average for the last three years of the survey, 61% of the female and 82% of the male respondents logged more than 40 hours. However, John Robinson, who has been studying the way Americans spend their time for 25 years, says his findings show a steady increase in free time.

Robinson, director of the Americans' Use of Time Project at the University of Maryland's Survey Research Center, has studied thousands of diaries that men and women have maintained on how they spend their time. Since 1965, he says, men have increased their free time per week from 34 to 41 hours. Women have gained six hours, from 34 to 40. Life may be much faster-paced, but we actually have more leisure time at our disposal. So why do we think we have less?

"The perception of a *time crunch* appears to have gone up in the period of time where free time has increased," says Robinson. In a 1991 study that he conducted for Hilton Hotels, he found that many people felt starved for time. Almost 50% of the 1,010 people interviewed said they would be willing to sacrifice a day's pay for an extra day off each week. The answers also indicated that women feel much more harried than men, especially if they have children and jobs, and that having a husband does not result in more leisure for these women.

"We are at a point," says Robinson, "when the value of time to most Americans is reaching parity with the value of money."

But what of compulsive overworkers, as in "workaholics," who seem to have increased in number during the last decade? Comparing the first three years with the last three years in table 2, male respondents working more than 40 hours per week are about the same in number: 83% in 1973-75, 82% in 1987-89. But in the later survey period, the percentages have shifted out of the 40-49 hour block and moved into the 50+. During the last three-year period, 32% of the men worked more than 50 hours, compared to 24% during the earlier period. Long hours on the job have intensified for women as well: 15% worked 50 hours or more per week during the last three years of the survey, compared to 6% during the first three years. What is the personal cost of all these hours on the job?

According to Diane Fassel, author of *Working Ourselves to Death: The High Cost of Workaholism and Rewards of Recovery,* consequences of workaholism include divorce, family break-up, stress-related illnesses, and eventually death. Any of these situations can seriously intrude upon one's sacred hours at the office; very few employees have been known to return from the dead for a luncheon meeting, no matter how important.

This does not apparently inhibit the compulsiveness of the typical senior executive. A 1991 Hyatt Hotel poll of 500 executives with incomes in excess of $125,000 reveals that almost 50% take work with them when they vacation. The average executive took 18 days of vacation per year, a period of time described as an opportunity to "prevent burnout, increase productivity on the job, and improve personal relationships." (Time to start rethinking that "I wanna be an executive" goal.) 70% said the office knows where they are at all times; 30% call in constantly (women and baby boomers were more likely to resent calling in); and 53% said they took shorter vacations as they climbed up the corporate ladder. 59% said they were happiest while on vacation; 60% said their sex lives improved dramatically.

"People want to feel their time off does something for them," says Marc Yanofsky, Hyatt's senior vice-president of marketing.

Q1: **Consider the following job characteristics:**
1) high income,
2) no danger of being fired,
3) working hours are short, lots of free time,
4) chances for advancement,
5) work important and gives a feeling of accomplishment. Among these five characteristics how would you rank "working hours are short, lots of free time?" NOTE: Question was not asked in 1972, 1975, 1978, 1979, 1981, 1983, 1986.

Responses: HI = Highest   NH = Next Highest   MD = Middle
NL = Next lowest   LO = Lowest

SEX	RESP	'73	'74	'76	'77	'80	'82	'84	'85	'87	'88	'89
F	HI	4%	5%	4%	5%	3%	3%	3%	3%	3%	2%	3%
	NH	10	12	8	8	8	9	6	7	8	8	7
	MD	13	12	12	10	11	14	9	9	11	10	7
	NL	25	25	22	25	26	20	22	20	26	27	23
	LO	48	45	54	53	53	54	59	61	53	53	61
# SURVEYED		783	779	799	811	801	320	853	824	807	561	550

SEX	RESP	'73	'74	'76	'77	'80	'82	'84	'85	'87	'88	'89
M	HI	6%	5%	4%	4%	4%	3%	3%	4%	5%	3%	3%
	NH	11	10	10	7	10	8	7	7	9	8	8
	MD	14	16	13	12	11	15	10	11	9	12	11
	NL	25	29	22	25	26	19	21	23	28	25	24
	LO	45	40	50	51	50	54	58	56	50	52	54
# SURVEYED		679	675	650	669	635	399	588	676	623	385	430

Q 2: How many hours did you work last week, at all jobs? NOTE: Question not asked in 1972.

Responses:	0 - 9	10 - 19	20 - 29	30 - 39	40 - 49
	50 - 59	60 - 69	70 - 79	80+	

SEX	RESP	'73	'74	'75	'76	'77	'78	'80	'82	'83	'84	'85	'86	'87	'88	'89
F	0-9	3%	1%	3%	3%	2%	5%	2%	4%	3%	3%	5%	4%	3%	4%	3%
	10-19	13	13	11	10	7	9	9	8	7	6	5	6	8	7	6
	20-29	17	10	14	10	11	11	10	10	10	13	10	9	11	10	12
	30-39	22	18	20	23	19	22	16	24	24	17	18	18	17	16	17
	40-49	41	49	45	49	54	46	50	45	47	47	47	47	46	47	45
	50-59	2	6	4	3	4	4	5	5	5	8	7	8	8	9	12
	60-69	1	2	0	1	3	3	3	3	2	3	5	6	4	6	3
	70-79	0	0	1	0	1	1	1	1	1	2	1	1	2	0	0
	80+	0	0	2	1	0	0	1	0	1	1	2	1	1	1	0
# SURVEYED		308	294	333	305	389	384	364	429	430	455	421	382	442	443	433
SEX	RESP	'73	'74	'75	'76	'77	'78	'80	'82	'83	'84	'85	'86	'87	'88	'89
M	0-9	1%	1%	1%	1%	1%	0%	2%	2%	1%	1%	1%	1%	1%	1%	1%
	10-19	1	2	3	4	3	2	2	2	3	4	3	2	2	2	3
	20-29	4	5	5	5	2	3	6	4	4	5	7	4	7	4	6
	30-39	9	8	10	9	10	8	8	10	12	6	9	10	8	8	7
	40-49	57	62	58	56	59	57	55	53	51	53	50	47	51	52	48
	50-59	14	13	13	12	14	15	11	15	12	16	14	19	14	17	16
	60-69	8	5	7	9	7	6	9	10	10	8	9	9	11	9	11
	70-79	4	2	2	2	2	5	3	2	4	4	3	4	2	4	4
	80+	2	2	1	2	2	4	4	3	3	3	4	3	3	2	3
# SURVEYED		475	447	431	442	488	471	458	418	481	421	491	453	479	447	474

☛ Table 1: Females are even less likely to place short working hours at the top of their "most wanted" list, even though other studies show that women are typically more pressed for time because of multiple professional and family obligations.

☛ Table 2: Professor Robinson reports that people older than 65 have the most free time, falling just short of the amount they would like. This corresponds to the findings of our survey, which shows 67% of the 66+ age group working less than 40 hours per week.

☛ Table 2: Most harried age groups? 30-35, with 29% working 50 or more hours per week, followed by the 36-41s at 28%. 49% of the 30-35s and 53% of the 36-41s worked in the 40-49 hour range (averaged for last three survey years). Robinson's studies also find that time demands are greatest on people in their 30s and 40s.

We is better educated, but the gender gap continues

WHO HAS MORE EDUCATION?

If you think men were born using grandiose, ostentatious words, greeting each other with secret handshakes, and drinking excessively, think again. This behavior is learned at college, and men are still more likely than women to have attended one of these institutions of higher learning.

Overall, the percentage of Americans with a college education doubled during the past two decades, from 12% to 24%. But the gap between men and women who have some college continues. In 1972, men were more likely than women (15% versus 9%) to continue their education after high school. Today, 29% of men have at least an Associate/Junior College degree, versus 21% of women.

Older respondents are far less likely to be college grads: In 1989, 30% of the 36-41 age group had bachelor or graduate degrees, while only 15% of the 54-65 group had similar educational backgrounds.

Question 2 concerns the overall level of education: the trend is that educational levels are going up. During the first three years of the survey, 39% of the male and 36% of the female respondents had attained an educational level of 11th grade or less. During the last three years, the numbers improved considerably: 26% of the male and female respondents had halted their education at or before the 11th grade. And what about college? During the first three years of the survey, men were more likely to have attended one to four years of college (28% vs. 23%), an advantage that women closed only slightly by the last three years (32% female compared to 36% male).

Q1: Respondent's highest educational degree.

Responses:
SS = Less than High School   HS = High School
AS = Associate/Junior College   BA = Bachelor's
GR = Graduate

SEX	RESP	'72	'73	'74	'75	'76	'77	'78	'80	'82	'83	'84	'85	'86	'87	'88	'89
F	SS	41%	36%	33%	37%	37%	35%	33%	32%	30%	26%	27%	27%	29%	24%	25%	25%
	HS	50	52	54	50	51	53	53	52	53	55	54	54	54	55	55	54
	AS	1	2	2	2	1	2	3	3	4	3	4	5	3	5	4	6
	BA	7	8	9	8	8	8	8	10	8	12	11	10	11	12	11	11
	GR	1	3	3	3	3	3	2	3	5	4	3	3	4	4	5	4
# SURVEYED		799	794	793	819	826	833	887	825	864	908	874	846	849	817	842	874

SEX	RESP	'72	'73	'74	'75	'76	'77	'78	'80	'82	'83	'84	'85	'86	'87	'88	'89
M	SS	39%	38%	38%	34%	33%	35%	28%	28%	29%	27%	27%	27%	25%	24%	24%	18%
	HS	46	44	43	48	46	44	52	49	51	49	49	49	48	48	50	52
	AS	1	1	1	3	2	3	2	3	4	5	3	3	4	4	5	6
	BA	9	10	10	11	13	11	12	12	11	13	13	13	16	17	13	14
	GR	5	6	8	4	6	7	6	7	5	7	8	9	8	7	8	9
# SURVEYED		791	695	690	670	667	691	642	639	637	689	596	688	620	640	638	656

Q 2: Level of education respondent has attained.

Responses:
1 = No formal schooling
3 = 6th - 10th grades
5 = 12th grade
7 = 3rd - 4th college year
9 = 7th - 8th college year

2 = 1st - 5th grades
4 = 11th grade
6 = 1st - 2nd college year
8 = 5th - 6th college year

SEX	RESP	'72	'73	'74	'75	'76	'77	'78	'80	'82	'83	'84	'85	'86	'87	'88	'89
F	1	1%	0%	0%	0%	0%	0%	0%	0%	0%	0%	0%	0%	0%	0%	0%	0%
	2	6	5	4	4	5	6	4	5	4	3	4	3	3	3	3	1
	3	26	23	21	24	26	23	22	22	20	16	18	18	18	18	17	17
	4	8	8	6	9	6	8	7	6	7	9	6	6	8	5	7	7
	5	36	38	40	36	40	37	37	37	36	37	35	36	36	35	33	34
	6	12	13	13	14	10	13	15	14	15	15	18	18	16	20	19	19
	7	9	11	12	9	10	9	10	12	11	14	15	13	12	11	14	14
	8	2	2	3	3	2	4	3	3	4	4	4	4	5	6	5	5
	9	0	1	0	1	1	0	1	1	2	1	2	1	1	2	2	2
# SURVEYED		805	800	792	818	825	830	885	823	864	909	874	846	849	820	841	873

SEX	RESP	'72	'73	'74	'75	'76	'77	'78	'80	'82	'83	'84	'85	'86	'87	'88	'89
M	1	1%	1%	1%	0%	0%	1%	1%	0%	1%	0%	0%	0%	0%	0%	0%	0%
	2	9	8	6	6	6	6	5	5	5	4	4	4	5	5	4	4
	3	22	22	26	20	21	23	20	20	17	17	18	16	15	15	14	11
	4	7	7	6	8	6	7	4	5	6	7	7	7	7	5	7	5
	5	27	26	26	30	28	29	33	31	33	31	31	31	29	30	28	29
	6	15	17	16	16	17	13	15	14	17	17	13	15	16	16	19	21
	7	13	12	11	13	13	14	13	13	14	16	16	15	18	19	17	16
	8	4	4	6	3	5	5	6	8	3	6	6	8	6	8	5	9
	9	2	4	3	2	3	3	4	4	3	3	5	5	5	4	5	5
# SURVEYED		803	699	689	669	668	690	641	640	637	688	596	688	620	640	637	657

☞ Table 1: Males lead in the percentage of four-year college degrees; but the average annual male/female difference is less than 2%. When it comes to graduate school, though, approximately twice as many men hold advanced degrees.

☞ Table 1: The amount of people who did not finish high school is dropping dramatically, from 40% in 1972, to 22% in 1989. Some of this decrease is derived from the fact that as older people drop off the survey, they are replaced by younger respondents who are better educated.

☞ Table 1: The increase in male high school graduates is 5% from 1972 to 1989. For females the increase is about 2%. In spite of the male high school retention rate growing faster than females, females have maintained an average annual lead of five points in the percentage of people with high school degrees only.

☞ Table 2: Again, younger respondents are much more likely to have more education. 71% of the 60-65 age group had attained a 12th grade or less level, compared to 41% of the 30-35 (averaged over the last three years of the survey).

POLITICS
& CRIME

Maybe they've taken this *laissez-faire* thing too far

POLITICIANS DON'T CARE?

"Since a politician never believes what he says, he is surprised when others believe him." Charles De Gaulle

A majority of the women and men in the General Social Survey think public officials have bigger stakes in their own personal interests than in the public they serve. Where they get these notions we don't know. But they seem to have come to this conclusion some time ago, and since the dark days of Watergate (1974) have averaged more than 65% who believe that politicians care little about the lot of the common guy and gal.

With the usual instant scandal brewing in Washington and elsewhere, such as Operation Abscam, the savings and loan bailout, and the Iran-Contra Affair, continued public cynicism seems assured. By 2070, nobody will trust them: in 1989, 7% more men and 6% more women expressed negative sentiment toward the attitudes of public officials than in 1973.

Of course, it's part of the grand American tradition to cast aspersions (asparagus?) at the moral fiber of our public officials. The big problem is locating that shifting moral fiber long enough to do some serious casting. Practice, however, makes perfect. American men and women have been at this a long time: we seceded from the English Empire because corrupt British politicians were becoming tiresome and we couldn't always understand them with those funny accents. And we had that slight geographic problem of having an ocean between us, making informal visits impossible. We wanted our own native shysters to take advantage of us. And we've succeeded, with that typical

American can-do spirit, on an extraordinary level. Jesse Helms. Richard Nixon. Joe McCarthy. Oliver North (hey, we didn't elect him!). Ronald Reagan. The Keating Five (a basketball team?). And thousands of other pols guilty of a million little (and some very big) indiscretions while feeding off a gullible public.

Respondents' displeasure with their politicians is increasing: comparing the first three with the last three survey years, 3% more male (64 to 67%) and 5% more female respondents (64 to 69%) have expressed the belief that politicians are not interested in their constituency, except to gather the required votes so that they can continue ignoring the constituency.

"I once said cynically of a politician, He'll double-cross that bridge when he comes to it.'" Oscar Levant

Although the gender gap is a slender 2%, slightly more women believe that most politicians are up to their (pick one suitable anatomical part) in self-interest. Perhaps this is due to the feminine gender's heightened feelings of symbolic disfranchisement, which is what happens when the beloved neighborhood diner is replaced by a McDonald's. Perhaps women feel more alienated from the government since it is largely run by men, and it seems on occasion, only for men. However, if more women were politicians, we'd guess that more women would be more critical of more women politicians.

Lucky for everyone involved, American men and women expect the worst from their politicians, who deliver with admirable consistency. Public cynicism is at an all-time high: a 1990 *New York Times* survey of 1,000 adults nationwide discovered that 71% thought that members of Congress are more interested in serving the needs of special interest groups than in working for the people they represent.

A *New York Times*/CBS News poll based on telephone interviews with 1,422 adults in 1990 on the subject of financial corruption among members of Congress discovered that 40% of the respondents think at least half of Congress is financially corrupt, while more than 50% think that perhaps some members are corrupt. 44% disapproved of the way Congress is handling its job. 22% disapprove of unnecessary Congressional trips to the bathroom and 10% think that the paintings on the walls of the Capitol are in bad taste.

The *Los Angeles Times* queried 2,046 California adults and found that 53% for sure think that bribe taking is a relatively common practice for their nefarious state legislators. Of course, 64% believe that it makes perfect sense to continue living on a major fault line.

A 1990 *Boston Globe* poll concerning the governor's race in Massachusetts found that 81% believed the state government was seriously out of touch with the state's residents, but inexplicably becoming better connected with the citizens of Wyoming. 48% thought state government existed to serve politicians, while 13% (bless them) felt that the government serves all the people. We could go on...

"An honest politician is one who, when he is bought, will stay bought." Simon Cameron

So why do we elect them if they continue to do whatever they please, in spite of our most excellent and explicit instructions to the contrary? Ain't this a democracy or something? Actually, we've become a nation of voter dropouts. During national elections, some 85 million of us (we the people) do not vote. 44% of the poor, 50% of the single, and 24% of the young under 25 years of age avoid the voting booth like it was a dentist's office. A recent survey of 240 college students found that those with a satisfying sex life were more likely to be politically active. We therefore believe that a system that provides regular sex for everyone would encourage higher voter turnouts. However, many politicians think that they're giving the voters all they can handle right now. And what about local and state elections? Basically dress rehearsals for election workers. They'd do a lot better if they gave away stuff, like microwaves to the first 100 who show up to vote.

Q: **Please tell me whether you agree or disagree with this statement. Most public officials (people in public office) are not really interested in the problems of the average man.** NOTE: Question was not asked in 1972, 1975, 1978, 1979, 1981, 1983, 1986.

Responses: AG = Agree   DS = Disagree

SEX	RESP	'73	'74	'76	'77	'80	'82	'84	'85	'87	'88	'89
F	AG	61%	64%	67%	65%	74%	68%	70%	65%	69%	70%	67%
	DS	39	36	33	35	26	32	30	35	31	30	33
# SURVEYED		775	766	803	796	787	818	849	810	797	554	563

SEX	RESP	'73	'74	'76	'77	'80	'82	'84	'85	'87	'88	'89
M	AG	58%	67%	66%	65%	71%	69%	70%	66%	71%	65%	65%
	DS	42	33	34	35	29	31	30	34	29	35	35
# SURVEYED		692	678	660	676	634	622	582	672	627	385	431

☛ Each gender hit a percentage high for distrusting perfidious politicos in 1980, possibly as a result of Operation Abscam. 31 public officials were accused by the FBI of criminal activity involving bribery for legislative favors.

☛ But not Jesse Jackson: For the last three years of the survey, 80% of the black respondents (403 surveyed) thought politicians are basically self-interested.

☛ Public service announcement for aspiring politicians: The 18-23s are the most trusting age group, with a mere 60% (averaged for the last three years of the survey) who believe that politicians don't care about Joe and Mary Common Folks. Of course, they're least likely to vote as well.

I wanna be with a conservative tonight

WHO'S HOTTER:
CONSERVATIVES OR LIBERALS?

For women and men, the 1980s will not be remembered as the decade of the liberal. You may recall the 1988 presidential campaign, when politicians tried to pin "the L-word" on each other like a scarlet letter. Or the punk rock band called The Dead Kennedys who declared the sixties "finally over." Or the ex-CIA chief who was elected president of the United States.

These images sum up a decade in which Americans, both male and female, found conservativism a sexier option than liberalism. Over the course of the survey, an average 34% of men ranked conservatives in the 70-99 degree range, while only 26% thought liberals were that hot. Although women are more likely than men to rank liberals highly, they still prefer conservatives, too. During the same time period, 33% of women ranked conservatives in the 70-99 degree range, with only 28% opting for liberals.

The more temperate zones drew the masses: 46% of the male and 49% of the female respondents ranked their feelings about conservatives in the 50-69 degree range, more like a spring day than a summer scorcher.

Liberal weather had a similar moderate forecast: 46% of the male and 48% of the female respondents placed liberals in the 50-69 degree range.

Traffic jam in the middle of the road

WHICH WAY DO YOU POLITICALLY LEAN?

If you have difficulty telling our two main political parties apart, the reason may be that they're both gunning for the same voter: Mr. and Ms. Moderate, hailing from Centerville, USA.

Compared to other modern democracies, American political extremes are sparsely populated. When men and women take a stand on political issues, both sexes are most likely to stomp their feet down firmly in the middle. When Ms. Slightly Liberal meets Mr. Slightly Conservative, do they dream of the day that they'll cross the not-so-great divide? Combining the categories of slightly liberal, moderate, and slightly conservative for the last three survey years, we find it easy to locate 67% of the male and 70% of the female respondents.

Women are even more middle-of-the-road than men, permitting male respondents to dominate the top two liberal and bottom two conservative categories. For the life of the survey, women have led in the "moderate" category by an average of 7.5%. In the "liberal" and "extremely liberal" categories, males dominated from 1974 to 1980, with an average of 16%, compared to 12% for the female respondents. From 1980 on, the sexes take turns lifting the liberal banner, with both males and females averaging 13%.

Political events obviously influence how people describe their political leanings. Males appear to have been particularly frustrated by the Carter administration's special brand of moderate liberal conservatism, expressing it by becoming more admiring of the Reagan Revolution and more strongly endorsing conservative politics. From 1974 to 1980, the average annual male score in the two more extreme conservative categories was 16%. From 1980 on, the average was 19%. Women likewise show an increased appreciation for conservative politics: from 1974-1980, their average was 14%, and from 1980 on, 16%.

As far as political parties go, Democrats are usually identified as the liberal standard bearers, while Republicans are typically described as conservatives. For the 1990s, which party do women and men across America think is best equipped to run the country? We turn to the polls:

Party allegiance? A recent *New York Times*/CBS News poll of 1,557 adults found that 44% identified themselves as Republicans or leaned in that direction, and 46% leaned toward or identified themselves as Democrats. It also discovered that some 55% of the Republicans earned over $50,000 per year, compared to more than 50% of self-identified Democrats who earned less than $15,000 per year.

Who do we trust? A *Washington Post*/ABC News poll found that 56% of the respondents believed that Republicans can do a better job governing the nation in the next five years. 38% felt that the Democrats could be trusted more with the same task (1,518 surveyed). The percentages on which party would do a better job on various issues:

- Handling the homeless: 56% Democrat, 25% Republican
- Reducing the drug problem: 47% Republican, 28% Democrat
- Helping the middle class: 53% Democrat, 32% Republican
- Handling the nation's economy: 52% Republican, 33% Democrat

Nevertheless, another *Washington Post* poll in 1990 (756 surveyed) discovered that 63% thought the Republican party posed a danger to the country by going too far in assisting the rich and cutting needed government services. A 1990 *Boston Globe* poll of 1,000 voters revealed that a majority thought Republicans provide better leadership for strengthening the economy and combatting drugs. Democrats surpassed Republicans on all other issues, including dealing with the problems of the Middle East (55 to 24%), creating a fairer tax structure (46 to 27%), and protecting the environment (52 to 27%).

A 1990 survey published in *The Wall Street Journal* of 1,019 registered voters nationwide discovered that 47% of the voters (to 18% for Republicans) believe that the Democratic Party would do a better job helping the middle class. The voters also believe the Democrats would do a better job looking out for the poor, 60% to 10%.

It's so hard to tell who's doing what from this distance: a poll of 1,494 people who described themselves as registered voters (likely story) were asked what the Democrat-controlled Congress is up to. 61% of Democratic voters and 62% of all respondents were unable to give a response, although 2% were recorded as coughing.

Q: **We hear a lot of talk these days of liberals and conservatives. I'm going to show you a seven-point scale on which the political views that people might hold are arranged from extremely liberal – point 1, to extremely conservative – point 7. Where would you place yourself on this scale?** NOTE: Question was not asked in 1972, 1973, 1979, 1981.

POLITICS ▼ CRIME

XL = Extremely liberal   LB = Liberal
SL = Slightly liberal   MD = Moderate, middle of the road
SC = Slightly conservative   CS = Conservative
XC = Extremely conservative

SEX RESP	'74	'75	'76	'77	'78	'80	'82	'83	'84	'85	"86	'87	'88	'89
F XL	1%	3%	2%	2%	1%	2%	2%	1%	1%	3%	2%	2%	3%	3%
LB	13	10	11	11	8	9	10	9	10	12	9	11	12	12
SL	15	14	12	15	17	14	15	13	14	10	13	14	12	13
MD	42	45	45	42	41	45	43	44	43	42	44	43	39	43
SC	14	16	16	16	18	17	14	16	17	17	16	14	16	16
CS	11	11	13	11	13	12	13	15	13	13	13	13	15	12
XC	2	1	1	3	2	3	3	1	2	3	3	2	2	2
# SURVEYED	745	760	758	789	822	800	815	293	829	798	799	766	798	807

SEX RESP	'74	'75	'76	'77	'78	'80	'82	'83	'84	'85	"86	'87	'88	'89
M XL	2%	3%	3%	3%	2%	4%	3%	3%	3%	2%	1%	2%	2%	3%
LB	15	16	16	13	12	8	8	8	9	10	10	15	12	13
SL	14	14	15	15	17	16	15	13	11	14	13	13	15	14
MD	37	34	34	35	34	35	38	40	37	34	38	33	32	35
SC	17	18	16	18	19	20	15	20	23	21	19	21	19	19
CS	12	10	14	14	14	13	16	13	13	16	17	12	17	15
XC	3	4	3	2	2	4	5	3	4	3	3	2	2	2
# SURVEYED	665	637	643	664	613	629	614	477	581	664	602	612	618	635

☞ Males diminished their liberal support after 1976, hitting a low in 1982 of 11%, compared to 19% in 1975 and 1976. Since then, male liberal support has risen to recover much of the lost ground, hitting 15% in 1987 and 1989.

☞ Women also gave up liberal ground in the '70s, and regained it in the '80s. The average annual male/female difference in the top two liberal categories was 3%.

☞ On the conservative side, the average annual male/female difference was 2%.

☞ No myth: The older you become, the more conservative your politics. The 54+ age group is the most enthusiastically conservative, with 34% in the bottom three categories. Liberals scored highest with the 18-41 group, with 33% in the top three categories (averaged for the last three years). The 36-41 age group was the most liberal at 37%; the 54-59 most conservative at 40%.

☞ Numbers for the died-in-the-wool political purist have not changed much in two decades. In comparing 1974-76 averages with 1987-89 averages (for total population), support for the top two liberal categories shrunk from 16 to 15%. Support for the top two conservative categories rose from 14 to 16%.

That same New York Times poll found that 58% of the black respondents thought it was true or might be true that the government deliberately makes drugs easily available in poor black neighborhoods. 29% of the black respondents thought it was true or might be true that the AIDS virus was deliberately created in a laboratory in order to infect black people.

Q : **If your party nominated a black for President, would you vote for him if he were qualified for the job?** NOTE: Question was not asked in 1973, 1976, 1979-1981, 1984, 1987.

Responses: YES   NO

SEX RESP	'73	'74	'76	'77	'80	'82	'84	'85	'87	'88	'89
F YES	72%	84%	83%	77%	85%	88%	88%	84%	88%	83%	83%
NO	28	16	17	23	15	12	12	16	12	17	17
# SURVEYED	633	760	685	699	842	816	863	802	818	517	546
SEX RESP	'73	'74	'76	'77	'80	'82	'84	'85	'87	'88	'89
M YES	75%	82%	81%	78%	85%	86%	83%	86%	87%	81%	83%
NO	25	18	19	22	15	14	17	14	13	19	17
# SURVEYED	632	663	562	599	618	606	663	657	609	420	401

☛ Comparing this question with the survey on voting for a female candidate, we find both sexes about equal in willingness to vote for a black or a woman for the nation's highest office.

☛ The average annual male/female difference is a small 2%.

☛ The trend lines of the "yes" responses have about the same upward slope for both sexes. 4% more male respondents were willing to vote for a black candidate in 1986-1989 than in 1972-1975; 5% more females were willing to vote for a black candidate in the later period than the earlier one.

☛ The big years for "yes" responses were 1982-86, during which they rose as high as 87%. Responses declined in the 1988 and 1989 surveys, to 82 and 83%.

☛ The age group most enthusiastic to a black candidate is the 24-41, averaging an 89% approval during the last three survey years. Least receptive was the 60+, averaging 76%.

Everyone seems to think so

ARE WE READY FOR MS. PRESIDENT?

A Gallup poll in the 1930s revealed that an underwhelming 34% of American men and women would vote for a female candidate and that no one had ever heard of cable television. Baby, we've come a long way since. 78% of the public has cable TV and 86% of the population now supports the notion of voting for a woman to fill the highest office in the land.

Yet for the life of the survey, men have been more supportive of the idea of a female president than have women. From 1972 to 1989, 84% of the men said they would vote for a woman prez; 82% of the women agreed. Remarkably, in only two of the 11 years this question was asked (1983 and 1989) did more women than men say they would vote for a female presidential candidate!

What does this prove? That men are more politically liberated? That people are less than honest during surveys? That a 2% difference is not a big deal; that the big deal is 8 of every 10 people are open to a woman running for president?

That women can run national governments at the same chaotic level as men has already been proven. The world has a handful of female heads or near heads of states; among them, Mrs. (Mary) Robinson, President of Ireland; Edith Cresson, the Prime Minister of France; President Corazon Aquino of the Philippines. Former British Prime Minister Margaret Thatcher was one of the world's most controversial leaders. Indira Gandhi, prime minister of India through three decades, was one of the more powerful leaders of our time. Benazir Bhutto was the first women to govern a Moslem nation. It would appear to be only a matter of time until a woman governs the U.S.

And that time could be any moment: the average for respondents aged 18 to 47 for the last three survey years was an awe-inspiring 92% in favor of female candidates.

Finding the right trail-blazing candidate is the hard part. Politics is a fickle business; you glad-hand, smile, kiss babies, stab your enemies behind their back, smile, glad-hand, deliver vague messages in a persuasive manner, promise more than you can ever deliver, and inspire others by noting the disappointing records and personality flaws of your opponents. Given that, who do we have as candidates?

A 1990 *McCall's* survey asked 7,000 women to rank their favorites female presidential candidates. American Red Cross president Elizabeth Dole came in first, followed by Democratic Congresswoman Pat Schroeder, Republican Senator Nancy Kassebaum, Texas governor Ann Richards, former San Franciscan mayor Diane Feinstein, and Kay Orr, the first elected woman governor in American history. 35% said they would prefer voting for a woman and 25% would rather vote for a man. 78% believe that an election should be decided on an individual basis and not because it is an important social goal to have women and minorities in office.

What about the generation coming of age now? A 1990 survey of 500 female college students on 16 campuses across the country revealed that only 8% wanted to be president. 79% agreed that a woman should be president and 64% believe that an African American woman should be president.

Q: **If your party nominated a woman for President, would you vote for her if she were qualified for the job?** NOTE: Question not asked in 1973, 1976, 1979, 1981, 1984, 1987.

Responses: YES   NO

SEX RESP	'72	'74	'75	'77	'78	'82	'83	'85	'86	'88	'89
F YES	74%	80%	79%	77%	80%	86%	87%	80%	84%	86%	88%
NO	26	20	21	23	20	14	13	20	16	14	12
# SURVEYED	771	762	793	809	864	839	885	820	825	531	554

SEX RESP	'72	'74	'75	'77	'78	'82	'83	'85	'86	'88	'89
M YES	74%	80%	82%	82%	83%	86%	86%	85%	89%	90%	84%
NO	26	20	18	18	17	14	14	15	11	10	16
# SURVEYED	762	671	650	675	628	617	661	661	602	427	399

☛ The average annual difference between the sexes is 3%, with men increasing their support by 9% and women by 8% over the course of the survey.

☛ Note that one year after Americans had an opportunity to vote for a female vice presidential candidate in 1984, support for the idea took a dip: a slight 1% for men but a 7% decline for women. The decrease in 1986 followed the indictments of Geraldine Ferraro's husband and son. Apparently women were not thoroughly comfortable with Ferraro as a role model. Ferraro is currently running for senator in New York.

☛ Both gender's responses seem sensitive to national issues of the time: consider the surge in support for women after the Watergate scandal in 1973, with both sexes jumping 6% in favor of women chief executives.

☛ Young boomers (Age 30-35) showed the highest level of support, averaging 94% for the last three survey years. The smallest vote of support came from the 66+ group, with 74% in favor.

☛ Black and white respondents were in synch: for the last three years, 87% of both black and white respondents said yes, we would vote for a female candidate if she was qualified.

Please, just make the world go away

ARE WE SPENDING TOO MUCH ON FOREIGN AID?

The U.S. (Big Daddy) supports much of the world with dollars, imposing so-called stability by enriching the coffers of shaky governments elsewhere. This is called peace through our prosperity. We also like to give away money to gain "influence" in the affairs of other countries, as we go about practicing world government (and the art of unintended consequences) by threatening to kill the golden goose unless we get our way.

Jamaica, for instance, is not a critical foreign area in most respects, but they do produce a lot of marijuana, a crop that the Bush administration would love to see go up in smoke. In 1991, Jamaica will receive about $65 million in U.S. aid, more than any other Caribbean country. In return, we've asked them to torch their marijuana fields; last year, 3,806 acres were burned and 58,000 pounds of pot were seized. Production has been cut 75%. Unfortunately, the shortage of *ganja* on the streets of Jamaica has led to an escalating number of crack cocaine users, a more severe social problem than a bunch of dreadlocked reggae fans smoking spliffs. Three treatment centers have opened in Kingston alone this year.

This is just one small example of the tangled financial web we weave. A bigger example is the millions in money (and weapons) we gave our good friend Saddam Hussein, helping finance his victorious march on Kuwait. Even the Soviet Union, no slouch at recognizing a good thing, wants our money.

The hard way, we've learned that money can't buy happiness or love or even reasonable security. Not that this lesson will affect our behavior. And if the U.S. government was run like a business, America would be out of business.

So it comes as no surprise that of all the government spending issues, foreign aid is the one most likely to have John Q. Public yelling "Too much." Although American women and men are generous in times of plenty, a sky-rocketing national debt and a menu of urban ills have caused many to say that charity must begin at home. About 75% of the population agrees that we are spending too much overseas, a degree of unanimity that is seldom found in this type of survey.

Men are typically less willing to part with American dol-lars for foreign aid, while women are less willing to sup-port defense expenditures. Over the course of the survey, the percentage of female respondents opposing the cur-rent level of foreign aid spending declined, from 76% dur-ing the first three survey years to 70% in the last three. Men were more eager to hang on to their wallets, showing a 1% decline (77 to 76%) in the bottom category.

Q: **We are faced with many problems in this country, none of which can be solved easily and inexpensively. I'm going to name some of these problems, and for each one I'd like you to tell me whether you think we are spending too much money, or about the right amount. Foreign aid.** NOTE: Question was not asked in 1972, 1979, 1981.

Responses: TL = Too little   AR = About right   TM = Too much

SEX	RESP	'73	'74	'75	'76	'77	'78	'80	'82	'83	'84	'85	'86	'87	'88	'89
F	TL	4%	3%	6%	3%	4%	5%	7%	5%	4%	3%	7%	7%	8%	5%	5%
	AR	23	18	19	20	26	26	21	19	19	23	27	23	23	25	28
	TM	73	79	76	77	70	69	71	76	77	74	65	70	69	70	67
# SURVEYED		743	746	767	781	767	822	771	812	850	234	298	404	241	398	401

SEX	RESP	'73	'74	'75	'76	'77	'78	'80	'82	'83	'84	'85	'86	'87	'88	'89
M	TL	5%	3%	6%	3%	4%	4%	3%	6%	4%	6%	6%	6%	7%	6%	4%
	AR	19	18	16	17	24	24	20	18	16	20	24	16	18	21	17
	TM	76	78	78	80	72	72	77	76	79	74	70	79	75	74	79
# SURVEYED		678	676	649	657	654	622	618	619	659	228	420	294	221	281	314

☛ World issues galvanize the public: In 1985, the year after President Reagan sent $45 million in famine relief to Ethiopia, approval of increased spending rose by 4% for women, while an additional 4% slid into the "just right" category. Men were less moved; increased spenders stayed at the 1984 level, while the "just rights" increased by 4%. By 1986, men and women were exhausted from making humanitarian gestures, with the "too much" category showing sharp increases for both sexes, no doubt spurred on by Reagan's request for $100 million in aid to the Nicaraguan Contras.

☛ The younger the group, the more supportive of foreign aid it was. For the last three survey years, 26% of the 24-29 age group said our spending was "about right," while 9% said it was "too little." In contrast, 84% of the 60-65 age group said our spending was "too much" for their tastes, 14% said the spending was fine, and a measly 2% believed it was "too little."

☛ Black and white respondents are basically in agreement about foreign aid. For the last three survey years, 22% said our spending was "about right." 9% of the black respondents think that the U.S. is not spending enough, compared to 5% of the white respondents. However, black and white respondents were only 2% apart in the top category during 1989 (6 to 4%).

Let's see those smart bomb videos again

BEST DEFENSE
IS AN EXPENSIVE DEFENSE?

"Nations have recently been led to borrow billions for war; no nation has ever borrowed largely for education. Probably, no nation is rich enough to pay for both war and civilization. We must make our choice; we cannot have both." Abraham Flexner, 1930

"To be prepared for War is one of the most effectual means of preserving peace." George Washington, 1790

The big story here is the 1980 spike that nearly doubled both male and female willingness to spend money on defense. You may recall that 1979 had been a dreadful year for America. In November, Ayatollah Khomeini's revolutionary guards took over the American embassy in Teheran, holding 52 Americans hostage in Iran, and the rest of America hostage in long gas lines. Emotionally, the country felt rather powerless; this event prompted 65% of males and 57% of females to favor increasing the military budget in order to bomb The Ayatollah into a better frame of mind. The failed helicopter rescue attempt in 1980 (after the survey was taken) only intensified Americans' feelings of embarrassment, fury, and impotence.

Ronald Reagan expertly exploited these feelings to defeat Jimmy Carter, who was perceived to have let down America's guard. Over the next eight years Reagan initiated the largest peacetime military buildup in history, nearly tripling the federal debt and deflecting money from many social programs in the process. By the end of the cold war in 1989, support for cuts in the defense budget was growing. Yet just as the debate about how to spend the "peace dividend" hit full steam, Iraq invaded Kuwait and derailed the movement toward defense cuts.

Defense spending now accounts for more than 25% of the federal budget. What's more, Americans have been increasingly willing to use the guns we have bought with our borrowed money. Since the hostages were released, military actions against Lebanon, Grenada, Libya, Panama, and, most recently, Iraq have received widespread approval and sent presidential popularity rates soaring. There's nothing like a good war to get America back on track

"A war regarded as inevitable or even probable, and therefore much prepared for, has a very good chance of eventually being fought." George F. Kennan, 1977

"Of the four wars in my lifetime, none came about because the U.S. was too strong." Ronald Reagan, 1980

Q: **We are faced with many problems in this country, none of which can be solved easily and inexpensively. I'm going to name some of these problems, and for each one I'd like you to tell me whether you think we are spending too much money, or about the right amount. The military, armaments and defense.** NOTE: Question was not asked in 1972, 1979, 1981.

Responses: **TL = Too little**   **AR = About right**   **TM = Too much**

SEX	RESP	'73	'74	'75	'76	'77	'78	'80	'82	'83	'84	'85	'86	'87	'88	'89
F	TL	11%	16%	14%	21%	23%	26%	57%	29%	22%	18%	16%	16%	15%	14%	14%
	AR	52	54	53	51	54	50	31	39	45	48	43	42	43	44	47
	TM	38	29	33	28	23	23	12	32	33	34	41	42	42	42	39
# SURVEYED		730	712	739	745	740	796	746	799	832	240	297	398	242	385	396

SEX	RESP	'73	'74	'75	'76	'77	'78	'80	'82	'83	'84	'85	'86	'87	'88	'89
M	TL	13%	20%	22%	31%	29%	33%	65%	33%	30%	18%	14%	18%	15%	21%	17%
	AR	44	43	44	38	44	43	23	36	34	37	44	39	42	40	38
	TM	43	37	34	31	27	24	12	31	36	45	42	43	43	39	45
# SURVEYED		677	668	648	650	664	617	624	627	674	229	425	293	221	287	325

☞ Male/female differences were clear, with more men in favor of increased defense spending every survey year except two (1984 and 1987) when the sexes tied and one (1985) when women took a two-point lead. The average annual difference between men and women is 5%.

☞ A *New York Times* poll published in January of 1990 found that 50% of the respondents felt that federal spending on military and defense should be kept the same.

☞ In spite of the one enormous fluctuation in 1980, the difference between the average of the first three survey years and the average of the last three survey years was less than 1% for both sexes.

☞ Most militant age group for the last three survey years? The 60-65, with 22% who believe that the U.S. is spending "too little" on the military, followed closely by the 48-53s at 21%.

☞ Age group with most pacifists? 30-35, with 49% who feel we spend too much on guns.

Do the right thing

SPENDING A CURE FOR BIG CITY ILLS?

Welcome to Jungleland: Students searched for weapons by security police and metal detectors. Teachers fearful for their own physical safety. Children murdered for jackets and shoes. Dropouts on the street, unable to compete. Crackheads and junkies littering the landscape. Break-ins and muggings just part of the scene. Suburban flight and urban ills. Homeless staying warm on street grills. No promise, no future, no today, no tomorrow.

Hey buddy, you got a dollar? No, I don't; overall, support for increased spending to solve(?) urban ills is declining, although the trend appears once again to be on the upswing. Support for bailing out big cities dropped between the first three survey years (1973-1975) and the last three (1987-1989). In the latter period, 7% fewer men and 5% fewer women were willing to spend more. A corresponding jump in the "about right" category has occurred, with female respondents increasing their average from 31% to 35% and male respondents making the larger leap into urban economy, from 29% to 37%. From 1987 to 1988, however, both men (7%) and women (10%) showed a sharp incline in the category "too little."

The list of urban problems is lengthy; many of our biggest cities are in big trouble, putting pictures on the television news that nobody wants to see and many chose not to. Those of us who don't live in the big city somehow are able to draw the line; it's them, not us, that have problems. Maybe it's easier because our largest urban areas are now dominated by minorities: Hispanics in Miami, Hispanics and blacks in L.A. and New York, blacks in Detroit, Atlanta, Chicago. Or maybe it's because the problems seem to dwarf our ability to solve them. Perhaps the big city has outlived its usefulness and is dying a natural death of attrition. But it promises to be a loud and tragic death. For the most part, women are more willing than men to spend more money on urban problems, averaging 53% from 1985-89 who think we spend "too little" on urban areas. Men averaged 44% for the same period.

It seems that when people feel gross mismanagement by city officials is at the heart of city troubles, as in the case of New York City in 1975, they are the least willing to help the residents of those cities or any other cities for a period of time thereafter. Men and women both increased their opposition to more federal spending over the next four survey years following NYC's federal bailout. From 1975 to 1980, female responses in the "too much" category leapt from 10 to 20%, and males increased their opposition from 19 to 30%.

Where do we go from here? In 1990, a *New York Times*/WCBS-TV poll asked New Yorkers what they thought about the future of the city. 59% wanted out of the city within four years; 64% said the economy would be getting worse. 60% of the Hispanic, 55% of the white, and 39% of the black respondents said the city would be a worse place to live in 10 or 15 years. A 1990 *Time*/CNN revealed that 68% of 1,009 New York City residents believe the quality of life in New York City is going downhill. 59% would move somewhere else if they could. While New Yorkers were happy in 1975 that the federal government saved their city from default, it didn't play as well in Peoria. If a similar situation occurred today, residents might opt to let the city go belly up, so long as they already had charted their escape path.

And what about Cleveland? The "Mistake by the Lake" did go into default in the 1970s, the first city to do so since the Great Depression. By 1983, Cleveland's unemployment rate was 11.3%, a 7% jump from 1978. But Cleveland has made a comeback, saved by a council of government and business leaders and an attitude of cooperation and free enterprise. The CEOs made 650 recommendations to government, 500 of which were quickly adopted. A number of self-help groups for entrepreneurs and civic promotional groups were formed, geared to get the good word out on Cleveland. Downtown bloomed as new businesses moved in and the lakefront and riverside areas were revitalized. Unemployment is down to the 6% level. While the commercial activity is a welcome change, Cleveland developer Albert Ratner says, "The real thing that changed is people's heads."

Q: **We are faced with many problems in this country, none of which can be solved easily and inexpensively. I'm going to name some of these problems, and for each one I'd like you to tell me whether you think we are spending too much money, or about the right amount. Solving the problems of big cities.** NOTE: Question was not asked in 1972, 1979, 1981.

Responses: TL = Too little   AR = About right   TM = Too much

SEX	RESP	'73	'74	'75	'76	'77	'78	'80	'82	'83	'84	'85	'86	'87	'88	'89
F	TL	56%	60%	60%	51%	48%	47%	48%	51%	51%	51%	51%	54%	47%	57%	57%
	AR	33	29	30	31	33	36	31	30	35	40	36	31	39	33	33
	TM	11	11	10	18	19	17	20	19	15	10	13	15	14	11	9
# SURVEYED		686	649	659	708	700	761	707	719	754	209	274	374	207	357	361

SEX	RESP	'73	'74	'75	'76	'77	'78	'80	'82	'83	'84	'85	'86	'87	'88	'89
M	TL	54%	57%	52%	45%	45%	40%	43%	48%	45%	51%	40%	40%	43%	50%	49%
	AR	29	28	29	28	28	31	28	25	33	31	38	38	40	37	34
	TM	17	15	19	26	27	28	30	27	22	19	23	22	18	14	16
# SURVEYED		633	609	582	610	611	573	571	572	619	213	387	277	199	251	298

☛ From 1975 to 1976, the percentage of men who said we are spending "too much" leapt from 19 to 26%. The percentage of women with this response went from 10 to 18%. These percentages stayed high until 1983, when they started a decline that would bring them down to 16% (male) and 9% (female).

☛ The average annual male/female difference was 6%.

☛ Women consistently led in the "too little" category, except during 1984 when an equal percentage of men and women thought "too little" was being spent.

☛ Big difference between black and white respondents' answers: for the last three survey years, 69% of the black respondents said America is spending too little on the cities; 47% of the white respondents concurred.

**Johnny can't read
and his school system's broke**

INVESTING IN THE FUTURE? SPENDING FOR EDUCATION

When it comes to saving our failing public school systems, most Americans are ready to put their money where their mouths are, a practice not in the best interest of sanitation. Over the last three survey years, a rapidly growing majority of men (65%) and women (67%) feel it's time to finance improvements in our education system. In fact, among the "spending" issues, education ranks with the leaders: fighting crime and drugs, protecting the environment, and providing health care. It may be high time too; 76% of 206 chief executive officers surveyed in 1990 said the public schools have worsened the U.S. workforce; 64% said improving public education is the most important factor for improving said workforce.

Not surprisingly, Americans are most willing to spend money on the kids in their own neighborhood. A 1990 CBS News poll found that 71% of Americans were willing to spend $100 a year more in taxes to help their local schools. Yet only 41% were willing to spend the same amount to "help schools anywhere." Respondents to this poll also felt that George Bush is all talk and no action as the "education president." 76% of the respondents to the 22nd annual Gallup/Phi Delta Kappa poll said it is unlikely or very unlikely that President Bush will reach his stated goal: by the year 2000, every school in America will be free of drugs and violence and will offer a disciplined environment conducive to learning. A nationwide survey conducted by the Roper Organization of 1,003 adults found that 91% of all respondents, and 96% of respondents who were parents which children in public schools, were somewhat or very concerned about the quality of their local schools. 51% said the quality of public education has declined in the past few years.

Let's hope that more money and improved resources will create a better educated student; the National Assessment of Educational Progress (NAEP) reports that while students are now more proficient in math, science, reading, and writing than they were 10 or 15 years ago, many of them perform well below their grade level in all of these subjects. For instance, 61% of 17 year-olds tested do not read well enough to understand the textbooks they're likely to encounter in high school. Almost 50% cannot understand junior high math, which is above the heads of many adults as well. 64% of 9 year-olds read as well as they should. Only 21% have the equivalent math skills. And it's not lack of money that troubles the schools most. The number one problem cited by the majority (31%) of the teachers queried is *lack of parental interest.*

On the other hand:

A poll by the Gallup organization of 231 semifinalists in the Thanks to Teachers competition revealed that the majority (40%) thought insufficient funds for supplies and materials was the major barrier in the way of effective teaching. 39% believed insufficient preparation time was critical. 86% said having a personal computer would help a great deal toward doing their job.

And teachers are increasingly unhappy; a survey by the Carnegie Foundation for the Advancement of Teaching involving 21,000 elementary and secondary public school teachers revealed that 45% are unhappy with the amount of control they have over their professional lives, while nearly 70% said they are only slightly or not at all involved in setting policies for student promotion and retention. Many of the more urban dwelling also resent being physically threatened by students, resorting to such old-fashioned methods of discipline as, "I've got a gun and I know how to use it."

Q: We are faced with many problems in this country, none of which can be solved easily and inexpensively. I'm going to name some of these problems, and for each one I'd like you to tell me whether you think we are spending too much money, or about the right amount. Improving the nation's education system.
NOTE: Question was not asked in 1972, 1979, 1981.

Responses: TL = Too little   AR = About right   TM = Too much

SEX	RESP	'73	'74	'75	'76	'77	'78	'80	'82	'83	'84	'85	'86	'87	'88	'89
F	TL	51%	52%	54%	54%	51%	55%	56%	61%	62%	63%	65%	64%	64%	68%	69%
	AR	41	40	38	37	41	36	35	33	33	35	31	33	30	29	29
	TM	8	8	8	9	8	9	9	7	5	2	4	3	6	3	3
# SURVEYED		758	753	773	794	794	846	784	824	869	245	307	409	249	402	419

SEX	RESP	'73	'74	'75	'76	'77	'78	'80	'82	'83	'84	'85	'86	'87	'88	'89
M	TL	51%	53%	48%	49%	48%	52%	53%	54%	62%	67%	60%	60%	63%	63%	70%
	AR	38	37	36	40	40	33	34	34	31	29	33	34	31	32	26
	TM	11	10	16	11	12	14	13	11	7	5	6	6	6	5	3
# SURVEYED		676	665	647	655	675	626	620	621	675	230	417	296	220	286	322

☛ The average annual male/female difference is 3%.

☛ In the "too little" category, the upward trend over time for both sexes is dramatic. In 1973, 51% of both men and women cited education as an area in need of more money. By 1989, this category had grown to include 70% of men and 69% of women.

☛ When the average of the first three years is compared with the average of the last three years we find that 15% more men and women chose "too little" money being spent.

☛ 70% of black and 66% of white respondents agree that we are spending too little.

☛ Age group most opposed to spending more on education? The 66+, with 55% voting too little. Most enthusiastic proponent of spending more? The 36-41, with 76% in category one. (Averaged for last three survey years.)

**50 ways to leave your lover
or save the planet**

ARE WE SPENDING ENOUGH TO KEEP THE PLANET GREEN?

"Once you've seen one redwood, you've seen them all."
Ronald Reagan, 1976

"For this generation, ours, life is nuclear survival, liberty is human rights, the pursuit of happiness is a planet whose resources are devoted to the physical and spiritual nourishment of its inhabitants." Jimmy Carter, farewell address, 1981

In all 15 of the survey years, more than 50% of the survey respondents – men and women alike – were willing to allocate more of the federal budget to improving and protecting the environment. But in 1973-74, the environment became a major concern, spurred by tales of smog alerts, car exhaust murk, pesticide poisoning, and, most of all, the national energy crisis (remember the Arab oil embargo?). 65% of the male and 63% of the female respondents said we were spending "too little" on the environment. That the environment was the hot story was fitting, for the planet was heating up as well, courtesy of the yet unnamed greenhouse effect or from a very long-term Bahamian high-pressure zone.

But starting in 1975 and in spite of the Carter administration's determined focus on conservation, concern fizzled for the remainder of the decade, with "too little" averaging 53% for men and 55% for women. Big tankers spilling oil failed to grab our attention: the tanker *Argo Merchant* ran aground off Nantucket in 1976, spilling more then seven million gallons of oil into commercial fishing grounds. A large oil spill from the supertanker *Amoco Cadiz* in 1978 destroyed fishing off the coast of France. Toxic chemicals didn't grab us: chemical waste turned Love Canal into a ghost town in 1978. Spending money at the pump didn't make us think twice: gas prices were rising. Nope, we just didn't want to pay attention.

Ironically, it was during the Reagan administration that environmental awareness erupted, rising, phoenix-like, from the sludge of one too many giant oil spills, the greed of reckless corporate polluters, and the lack of interest by the administration in creating a public policy that might some-how balance our need for economic development with the equally pressing requirement to preserve some land, somewhere, for our children. From 1980 to 1984, 13% more male and 9% more female respondents said we were spend-ing "too little." The concern was also that it was "too late."

Today, environmental issues are near and dear to the hearts of many women and men. We've recognized the asbestos in the pipes overhead and have felt the toxic chemicals, not wings, beneath our feet. We accept that the ozone is disappearing, apparently an inadvertent casualty of mod-ern deodorant and hair spray application (but we do look and smell nicer); we read that the ice caps are melting, set-ting adrift countless penguins; we know that the land fills are full, with most of the garbage having the half-life of uranium; we watch on TV as barges loaded with rotting waste forlornly circle the globe, looking for a friendly port; and we indulge in recycling, the trendy, modern way of saying thank you, world. Think green, baby. Our envi-ronmental consciousness is reaching acute heights which may well translate into significant action during the '90s. And as time goes by Americans, particularly women, are becoming even more willing to spend that money. When the averages of the first three and last three survey years are compared, we find that 8% more men (62 to 70%) and 10% more women (61 to 71%) chose the "too little" response.

And at the next cocktail party, you'll be as unpopular as the captain of the Exxon Valdez if you insist that we're spending too much on the environment. In the first three survey years, an average of 12% of the male and 6% of the female respondents said we were spending "too much" on the environment. In the last three survey years, that percentage neatly declined by half for both sexes, to 6% for the men and 3% for the women.

A 1990 *New York Times*/CBS News poll with 1,557 adults discovered that 57% favored increasing federal spending on the environment. A survey commissioned by the Ford Motor Co. and published in *The Atlanta Journal and Constitution* queried 7,000 leaders in business, education, the media, government, and environmental advocacy. 80% believe that the public would be willing to pay more for environmentally safe products. 85% believe the federal government should take the lead in setting environmental standards; 70% are skeptical of private industry acting voluntarily to protect the environment; and 90% see the public's awareness of environmental issues growing "very rapidly" in the next few years.

Another recent survey (*Baltimore Sun,* 1990) found that almost 80% of Americans say more should be done to improve the environment, but less than 25% say they are actually doing something about it. It found that women are generally more environmentally aware, and that people with higher incomes are generally more involved than those who earn less. In a 1990 *Wall Street Journal* poll, 80% of Americans said it is more important to protect the environment than to keep prices down, a 29% increase from 1981.

Q: **We are faced with many problems in this country, none of which can be solved easily and inexpensively. I'm going to name some of these problems, and for each one I'd like you to tell me whether you think we are spending too much money, or about the right amount. Improving and protecting the environment.**
NOTE: Question was not asked in 1972, 1979, 1981.

Responses: TL = Too little   AR = About right   TM = Too much

SEX	RESP	'73	'74	'75	'76	'77	'78	'80	'82	'83	'84	'85	'86	'87	'88	'89
F	TL	65%	61%	58%	57%	50%	58%	53%	54%	58%	62%	57%	61%	69%	69%	75%
	AR	29	32	36	36	39	35	35	37	34	35	36	33	27	27	23
	TM	6	7	6	8	10	7	13	9	8	3	6	6	3	4	3
# SURVEYED		740	732	752	782	764	830	769	798	837	236	299	399	237	402	404

SEX	RESP	'73	'74	'75	'76	'77	'78	'80	'82	'83	'84	'85	'86	'87	'88	'89
M	TL	65%	65%	55%	58%	52%	51%	48%	52%	57%	61%	60%	66%	68%	66%	76%
	AR	26	25	30	30	34	34	31	32	33	33	30	28	25	29	20
	TM	10	10	15	12	14	15	21	16	10	6	10	5	7	5	5
# SURVEYED		673	646	646	643	650	618	613	609	657	230	418	283	220	283	327

☛ The gap between men and women on support for environmental spending has been as much as 7% (1978); but with that exception, the sexes have been close on this question most survey years. The average annual male/female difference of opinion on this issue is only 3%.

☛ For the last three survey years, black respondents in the "too little" category averaged 75%, compared to 70% for white respondents.

☛ The 24-41 age group is the most concerned about the environment, averaging 77% over the last three survey years who believe we are spending "too little."

☛ Least concerned is the 60+ group, averaging 59% who believe "too little." However, in 1989, the 60-65 age block showed a sharp jump in that category, from 56 to 73%, as did the 66+, from 52 to 60%.

I'd rather not...

SPEND MORE ON WELFARE?

Depending on your position, welfare is either...

A) A compassionate, civilized program that saves men, women, and children from dire poverty and misery, or...

B) A fraud-ridden free ride that encourages sloth and provides a disincentive to productive endeavors.

The war on poverty is over and we have lost. 12.8 million people are on public assistance, the largest number in U.S. history. Welfare is among the most divisive issues being debated today, although the lines are not drawn between the genders (overall, women typically support welfare spending only slightly more than men). Rather, the debate about welfare rages between the haves and have-nots, the liberals and conservatives, blacks and whites, country folks and city slickers. Over the life of the survey, male respondents averaged 19% in the "too little" category, while female respondents averaged 21%. In the "too much" category, the race was also close: 51% of the male and 49% of the female respondents believe we are spending excessive amounts on welfare.

Patricia Ruggles, senior research associate at the Urban Institute in Washington, D.C. and one of the country's leading experts on poverty measurements, doesn't expect the country's sympathies to change soon. "Some of it is a straight cultural shift," says Ruggles. "The Reagan era introduced the belief that materialism is a good thing, and if you're poor, it's your fault."

And how does this jibe with our present situation? Before the 1990 recession began, one of every eight Americans was living below the country's official poverty line—$13,360 for a family of four in 1990, which translates into 32 million people.

Although 45% of those who fall below the poverty line recover within a year, 12% remain impoverished for a decade or more, while the remainder struggle for long periods in between. An obstacle facing those attempting to lift themselves out of poverty is that unemployment insurance, food stamps, AFDC (Aid to Families with Dependent Children), and other public assistance programs are vulnerable to cuts in years of tight budgets and conservative administrations. For instance, in May of 1991, 303,000 people exhausted their unemployment benefits by being out of work more than 26 weeks, the most in one month since August 1983. Due to cuts in federal supplemental unemployment benefits, just 20% of those people live in states that qualify for extended federal benefits. 80% have only welfare.

Throughout the 15-year survey period, men and women have displayed much variation in opinions on this issue. During the Carter years (1976-80), opposition to increased spending reached a peak, with 59% of the female and 64% of the male respondents saying "too much." This coincided with a period of severe inflation coupled with Californian tax rebellion. In particular, farmers were hard hit, with many losing their businesses. During the Reagan era, concern on welfare spending decreased, due in part to the slashing of many social programs. From 1982 to 89, women averaged 45% and men 46% in the "too much" category.

Q : **We are faced with many problems in this country, none of which can be solved easily and inexpensively. I'm going to name some of these problems, and for each one I'd like you to tell me whether you think we are spending too much money, or about the right amount. Welfare.** NOTE: Question was not asked in 1972, 1979, 1981.

Responses: TL = Too little   AR = About right   TM = Too much

SEX	RESP	'73	'74	'75	'76	'77	'78	'80	'82	'83	'84	'85	'86	'87	'88	'89
F	TL	20%	24%	25%	15%	14%	15%	15%	22%	23%	26%	22%	26%	22%	26%	24%
	AR	27	35	31	26	25	26	29	30	29	33	35	31	28	32	32
	TM	53	42	44	60	61	58	56	48	48	41	43	43	50	42	44
# SURVEYED		753	754	753	780	792	853	785	825	865	244	303	405	246	399	409

SEX	RESP	'73	'74	'75	'76	'77	'78	'80	'82	'83	'84	'85	'86	'87	'88	'89
M	TL	21%	22%	25%	13%	12%	11%	13%	19%	21%	23%	17%	19%	22%	20%	24%
	AR	24	31	29	21	23	25	25	28	29	36	34	41	36	35	31
	TM	55	46	46	66	65	64	62	53	50	41	49	41	42	45	45
# SURVEYED		679	668	652	649	657	620	616	614	665	227	416	295	215	286	311

☛ The lowest point of positive opinion for welfare spending was 1978, when only 11% of males thought it was "too little." A comparison of the averages of the first and last three survey years shows a drop of less than 1% for men and an increase of 1% for women choosing the "too little" category.

☛ Statistical calculations make male/female differences appear fairly small (an annual average gap of only 3%), but in some years as much as 7% separated the sexes.

☛ For the last three survey years, 40% of the black respondents believe we are spending too little. A little more than half (21%) of the white respondents agreed.

☛ The 18-23, 60-65, and the 24-29 age groups are most in favor of increased spending. For the last three years, the 18-23s averaged 29% in the top category; the 60-65s, 28%; and the 24-29s, 27%.

☛ The 48-53 group had the highest percentage in the "too much" category, averaging 51% for the last three survey years. It was closely followed by the 42-47 and 30-35 at 49%.

Get sick, go broke, then die

IS IT TIME FOR NATIONAL HEALTH CARE?

For those who can afford it, health care in the United States is the best that money can buy. It is also the most expensive; the U.S. spends a higher proportion of its GNP on health care than any other country in the world. We are the only industrialized nation without a national health care system, and the only nation outside the Third World in which millions go without quality health care for financial reasons. Apparently, this strikes nerve in both genders. From 1987 to 1989, 66% of the male and 72% of the female respondents said the government was spending "too little" on health care. Support among women – more of whom hold part-time and low-paying jobs without health benefits – is growing at a rate faster than that of men, who actually have held steady in the "too little" category. From 1973-75, 66% of the male respondents said we were spending too little; females in category one averaged 64%. Males have shown greater movement in the "too much" category, averaging 6% in the first three and 3% in the last three survey years, after peaking at 12% in 1980.

Can people afford the cost of a major illness? The *Atlanta Journal and Constitution* polled 751 adults in 1990 on the question and discovered that 62% believe that they can. 4% are not sure, and 34% said no, I can't.

A survey sponsored by the American Association of Retired Persons (AARP) of 1,500 adults, of whom 500 were aged 18-49, 500 were 50-64, and 500 were 64 and over, found that 53% are not confident that they would be able to pay for long-term care. 73% believe that nursing home expenses would wipe out their savings.

Concern with national expenditures in health care cuts across age blocks. In the General Social Survey, 74% of the 60-65 age group said we were spending too little on health care (averaged for the last three survey years). Their level of concern was shared by the 36-41s, with 74%, the 42-47, at 75%, the 48-53, at 73%, and the 30-35, with 72%. The group least supportive of additional spending was the always surprising 66+, averaging 61% in the top category.

Apparently our senior GSS respondents don't belong to the American Association of Retired Persons. A recent *AARP Bulletin* survey of 70,000 readers found that 84% favored a government-sponsored national health insurance program. A Roper Organization poll of 100 business executives revealed that 94% opposed a national health plan, while 75% favor shifting more of the health costs to the employee. And although President Bush said in 1990 that the Health and Human Services Department would begin working on a national health program, 63% of 250 hospital chief executive officers do not think the President is personally committed to developing a new health policy.

In a related 1990 poll of 2,000 people nationwide by the Gallup Organization, 53% said they would be willing to pay more taxes to provide health care, and 68% said government spending on health care should increase. On the issue of national health care, 49% supported the idea and 43% said it would be a costly mistake. Another Gallup survey of 2,000 adults found that 73% favor government-provided health care, but significantly fewer respondents wanted it if it meant traveling farther to the doctor (43%), waiting longer for care (36%), or would restrict the choice of health care providers (29%).

73% of 1,004 Californians polled in 1990 would agree to higher taxes to pay for health care for the poor and uninsured. 50% "strongly agreed" and 34% "agreed" that employers should be required to provide basic health insurance to their employees.

Clearly, more women and men are recognizing that the long-term costs of ignoring health care will be substantially higher than the costs of addressing the issue today. This bodes well for supporters of a national health care plan and increased spending in health research.

Q: **We are faced with many problems in this country, none of which can be solved easily and inexpensively. I'm going to name some of these problems, and for each one I'd like you to tell me whether you think we are spending too much money, or about the right amount. Improving and protecting the nation's health.** NOTE: Question was not asked in 1972, 1979, 1981.

Responses: **TL = Too little**   **AR = About right**   **TM = Too much**

SEX	RESP	'73	'74	'75	'76	'77	'78	'80	'82	'83	'84	'85	'86	'87	'88	'89
F	TL	62%	65%	65%	62%	60%	58%	60%	59%	60%	63%	63%	65%	74%	70%	73%
	AR	34	31	31	34	34	36	35	34	35	32	31	33	22	26	25
	TM	4	4	4	4	6	6	5	6	5	4	6	3	4	4	3
# SURVEYED		765	753	775	792	784	844	784	812	867	237	310	410	252	409	416

SEX	RESP	'73	'74	'75	'76	'77	'78	'80	'82	'83	'84	'85	'86	'87	'88	'89
M	TL	64%	68%	66%	63%	57%	57%	53%	59%	59%	57%	57%	55%	64%	66%	68%
	AR	30	27	28	30	35	34	35	34	35	33	37	39	32	32	29
	TM	6	5	7	6	9	9	12	7	6	10	7	6	4	2	4
# SURVEYED		680	673	650	649	670	627	623	612	664	228	417	292	219	283	322

☛ The average percentage of males who support more spending for the last three survey years is about the same as the average of the first three years. Women, on the other hand, have increased their support by 8%.

☛ Black respondents favor increased spending by an average of 78% during the last three survey years. From 1973-75, the level of support was 75%. White respondents averaged 68% in the top category during 1987-89.

The Ts, the Els, and the Tubes are no match for a '73 Impala and a turnpike

MASS DOLLARS FOR MASS TRANSIT?

Unique among modern democracies, the USA is a place where women and men like to travel **alone** to work. By themselves. Singing to the radio. Drinking coffee and cokes. Talking on the telephone. Putting makeup on. Star gazing. Flirting. Fixing flats. The romance of the open road and the drive-through restaurant. Except for a handful of major cities, governments tend to stay out of the business of moving people around in groups. We believe mass transit is for cattle, pigs, chickens and other livestock desiring to see America by road, not for people who don't need people. Our excellent (though deteriorating) highways encourage the road warrior in every man and woman, and that do-your-own-thing spirit has made us perhaps just a little suspicious of communal transport: cramming more than one person in a car bound for work is esthetically unpleasing. Consequently, we're not particularly gung-ho about spending money for mass transportation.

While not quite as unpopular as spending more on welfare, increasing the mass transportation budget appears to be a cult thing. For the six survey years, females averaged 32% and males 36% in the "too little" category. Even after the rising fuel costs and shortages of the '70s and concerns about the environment in the 80s, minds and pocketbooks have have not changed much. In fact, at no time from 1984-1989 did support for mass transit threaten to become a majority item for either sex. Throughout the survey, women were especially unsupportive of more spending for mass transportation, while men's support fluctuated 10% or so.

Q: **We are faced with many problems in this country, none of which can be solved easily and inexpensively. I'm going to name some of these problems, and for each one I'd like you to tell me whether you think we are spending too much money, or about the right amount. Mass transportation.** NOTE: Question was not asked in 1972-1983.

Responses: TL = Too little   AR = About right   TM = Too much

SEX	RESP	'84	'85	'86	'87	'88	'89
F	TL	34%	30%	32%	33%	31%	30%
	AR	57	59	57	55	60	63
	TM	9	11	11	12	10	7
# SURVEYED		486	730	751	705	702	723
SEX	RESP	'84	'85	'86	'87	'88	'89
M	TL	41%	37%	31%	33%	34%	38%
	AR	43	47	53	50	53	49
	TM	16	17	17	17	14	13
# SURVEYED		395	642	574	590	575	596

☛ From 1984 to 1986, male support for increasing the mass transportation budget dropped by 10%. But two years later men were feeling positive again and support was up to 38%. We don't know why.

☛ Although mass transit is an environmental issue, respondents did not seem to make the connection. Or if they did, they dismissed it.

☛ For the last three survey years, 33% of the black and 32% of the white respondents are in favor of increased spending.

The open road should be pothole-free

FINANCE THE FREEWAY IMPROVEMENT PROGRAM?

Although both sexes would rather spend their tax dollars on highways than mass transit, men are most interested in turning America's highways and bridges into one large construction zone, obviously anticipating with delight those total gridlock moments that inspire uncharted detours into the heartland of America, satisfying the male yen for exploration without maps.

Women and men saw the need for highway spending before the debate over the 1986 bill authorizing the expenditure of over $40 million on highway improvements. When it became apparent that the highway bill would be passed, men and women nodded their approval, with 9% of the men and 6% of the women traveling from Too Little Blvd. to Just Right Ave. Leery of their new neighbors, 2% of the female residents on Just Right found new homes on Too Much St.

Since then, support for more highway spending has crept back up, but is still 2 to 3% below 1985 levels.

On the topic of road repair: what are the 10 worst roads in America? According to those gypsies of the interstates, the truck drivers?

1. I-80 in Iowa
2. I-70 in Kansas
3. I-84 in Kansas
4. I-40 in Arkansas
5. I-81 in Pennsylvania
6. I-90 in Ohio
7. I-10 in Louisiana
8. I-10 in California
9. I-94 in Illinois
10. I-80 in Pennsylvania

Q: **We are faced with many problems in this country, none of which can be solved easily and inexpensively. I'm going to name some of these problems, and for each one I'd like you to tell me whether you think we are spending too much money, or about the right amount. Highways and bridges.** NOTE: Question was not asked in 1972-1983.

Responses: **TL = Too little**   **AR = About right**   **TM = Too much**

SEX	RESP	'84	'85	'86	'87	'88	'89
F	TL	45%	41%	35%	33%	35%	38%
	AR	48	52	55	57	56	54
	TM	7	7	9	10	8	7
# SURVEYED		531	782	797	759	778	790
SEX	RESP	'84	'85	'86	'87	'88	'89
M	TL	53%	46%	38%	41%	41%	44%
	AR	40	45	54	52	52	48
	TM	7	9	8	7	7	7
# SURVEYED		405	666	596	614	618	638

☛ Throughout the course of the survey, less than 10% of the respondents thought we were spending "too much" on highways and bridges.

☛ The average annual male/female difference in the "too little" category is 6%.

☛ In 1989, the age group most concerned about losing wheel covers and damaging shock absorbers due to poor road maintenance was the 66+, with 51% saying spend more.

Not if you value your political life

CUT SOCIAL SECURITY SPENDING?

Let's see. According to the General Social Survey, environment is a priority spending item. So is education.

Health care, now that has a lot of public support. And we must have good roads. But what's that other priority spending issue? The one that really stirs up a tempest in a beehive?

Oh yes, Social Security.

Only a Congressman with a death wish or a tidy little retirement nest egg of his or her own would attempt to cut the funding for the Social Security program. Better to contend with the zealots at the National Rifle Association over gun control; you'll take less abuse. In fact, so many politicians have had their wrists slapped while messing with the Social Security program that today's word is "hands-off." Of course, challenging the program is a swell way of meeting great numbers of senior citizen pen pals.

Most men and women want to maintain or increase the current level of financial support for Social Security, and more are jumping on the bandwagon. In 1984, 90% of the adult population said the government was spending either the right amount or too little. In 1989, that number had grown to 96%.

Women are the true champions of Social Security, as they are for most human services issues. Over the six years of the survey, 9% more women (59%) than men (50%) favored Social Security spending increases. For many women, Social Security is potentially a meat and potatoes issue: they live longer past retirement age, often without spouses and often without a private retirement program. Social security may be the only economic safety net they'll have.

As expected, age was a factor in the "too little" category, but with a surprising twist. Those furthest, rather than closest, to retirement age showed the most support for increased spending. 62% of the 24-29, 60% of the 30-35, and 60% of the 36-41 age blocks said we should increase spending, on average, from 1987-89. During that same period, only(!) 49% of the 66+ and 53% of the 60-65 age groups selected category number one, locking them into statistical agreement with the youngest group, the unpredictable 18-23s, otherwise known as the sons and daughters of Eisenhower.

Q: **We are faced with many problems in this country, none of which can be solved easily and inexpensively. I'm going to name some of these problems, and for each one I'd like you to tell me whether you think we arc spending too much money, or about the right amount. Social Security.** NOTE: Question was not asked in 1972-1983.

Responses:	TL = Too little		AR = About right		TM = Too much	

SEX	RESP	'84	'85	'86	'87	'88	'89
F	TL	57%	56%	61%	60%	60%	61%
	AR	36	39	33	35	36	36
	TM	6	5	5	5	4	3
# SURVEYED		528	812	818	782	799	822

SEX	RESP	'84	'85	'86	'87	'88	'89
M	TL	48%	50%	51%	53%	48%	51%
	AR	39	40	41	38	44	43
	TM	13	9	8	9	8	6
# SURVEYED		394	669	601	611	607	632

☞ In the "too little" category, support is fairly steady across the life of the survey. The fastest growing segment is the female, with a 2% increase between the average of the first three and the last three survey years. Or a 3% increase between the first two and last two survey years. Or a 4% increase between the first and last years. If 1986 is compared with 1989, there is no difference at all. (Do not try this sort of statistical mastery while home alone.)

☞ Blacks were more likely to favor increases in Social Security spending (79% versus 54% of whites).

**I want to be a spaceman,
that's what I want to be**

ANY EXTRA BUCKS FOR SPACE EXPLORATION?

Our finding that men are the most likely supporters of space research won't surprise anyone who's been to a Star Trek convention and watched all those strange guys in short tight pants parade around in search of Dr. Spock, famous baby book author. Space is a macho and dangerous territory, the final frontier. And men, the traditional explorers in the family ("okay honey, I'll go look for it in the basement"), are thrilled to vicariously go where only 125 or so have been before, expertly using remote controls and an ordinary television set to get there. Men can relate to the power and shape of a rocket rising from the launch pad and likewise identify with all those stages falling limply back to earth. Men can explain why countdowns are important (so everyone pushes their buttons at the exact same time) and why they have those big padded shoulders in the astronaut suits (David Byrne fashion imitation).

In fact, men are willing to pay extra when they perceive a higher degree of risk. A bizarre case in point is the 1986 Challenger accident. Interest in space travel had been dwindling since 1980, but the disaster spurred a 12% surge in male support over the next two years. In 1989, support among both males and females dropped slightly, but overall, late-eighties levels of support were double those of the early seventies.

It should be noted that interest in space flight remains basically a white guy phenomenon. Black respondents are not much in favor of increasing the dollars available for exploring the heavens when so much remains to be done here on earth. During the last three survey years, 66% said that the current level is too high, while only 6% said spend more.

And the older you get, the less likely you are to fantasize about life as an astronaut or a Klingon. For the last three survey years, only 9% of the 66+ age set think spending more is appropriate, while 49% believed that the current level is excessive.

Q: **We are faced with many problems in this country, none of which can be solved easily and inexpensively. I'm going to name some of these problems, and for each one I'd like you to tell me whether you think we are spending too much money, or about the right amount. Space exploration program.** NOTE: Question was not asked in 1972, 1979, 1981.

Responses: **TL = Too little**   **AR = About right**   **TM = Too much**

SEX	RESP	'73	'74	'75	'76	'77	'78	'80	'82	'83	'84	'85	'86	'87	'88	'89
F	TL	5%	5%	4%	4%	6%	5%	14%	7%	8%	7%	7%	7%	11%	11%	7%
	AR	29	24	28	26	35	33	36	43	43	37	39	43	37	44	46
	TM	66	71	68	70	59	62	50	50	49	56	54	50.	53	46	46
# SURVEYED		754	755	777	802	773	818	739	803	840	232	301	399	232	393	401

SEX	RESP	'73	'74	'75	'76	'77	'78	'80	'82	'83	'84	'85	'86	'87	'88	'89
M	TL	12%	12%	12%	16%	16%	22%	27%	21%	23%	18%	15%	18%	24%	30%	26%
	AR	33	34	36	32	39	43	40	45	44	54	51	48	44	46	48
	TM	56	54	52	51	45	35	34	34	33	28	34	34	32	24	25
# SURVEYED		678	672	648	657	667	618	605	608	662	228	420	298	222	280	316

☞ Support for increased NASA funding was at its lowest during the first three years of the survey's history, averaging 12% for male and 5% for female respondents in the "too little" category. Females averaged a spectacular 68% in the "too much" category during this period, compared to 54% of the men.

☞ Male enthusiasm for the space program has always been far stronger than female support. The average annual male/female difference is a whopping 12%. One reason is that until recently, they never got to go on the ride. But male support has been more volatile, varying within a range of 18% (between 12% and 30%), while women have varied by only 7%.

☞ When the average of the first three years is compared with the average of the last three, we find that 15% more men (12% to 27%) said we are spending "too little" in our drive to become lost in space. Women were less enthusiastic about spending money in space while the malls were still open, with 5% more in the "too little" category (5% to 10%).

☞ More than 80% of men over the age of 25 who are living in their parents' basements said they "aspire to the lofty professional achievements of Captain James Kirk."

God save our hockey teams

OH, CANADA: HOW DO WE LOVE THEE?

The favorite country of most American women and men is Canada – by far. Some 80% give Canada a high ranking (from +3 to +5 on our scale).

Why such a favorable opinion of our northern neighbor? Well, the Canadians don't cause a lot of trouble in the world, preferring to leave that up to us. They have clean, safe cities, majestic wilderness, decent beer, and great hockey teams. On Saturdays, Canadians arm themselves with little brooms and curl. They have brave mounties and more savings accounts than people. But they pay $100 for a carton of cigarettes and only slightly less for a tank of gas. Out there in Alberta, where the Great Gretsky once skated, is the world's largest shopping mall, reportedly as big as Delaware but without the coastline. And a significant part of the country refuses to speak English and will not salute the Queen, except in an impolite way. Those things aside, they are a lot like us. Or we're a lot like them.

And though they hate to admit it, we love 'em for it.

A recent *MACLEAN'S* poll of 1,500 Canadians found that one in six would choose union with the United States if their province had the opportunity to become a state, with 27% of Newfoundland and 25% of Quebec inclined to support statehood. Nevertheless, the majority of Canadians feel they enjoy better health care, a higher quality of living and greater world respect than the people in the U.S. On the downside, only 36% felt their economy was better and only 22% thought their politicians were superior.

Q: On a scale that goes from "plus 5" for a country you like very much, to the lowest position of "minus 5" for a country you dislike very much, where would you rate Canada?

NOTE: 1972-1973, 1976, 1978-1981, 1984, 1987.

Responses: +5 = +5 +4 = +4 +3 = +3 +2 = +2 +1 = +1
           -1 = -1 -2 = -2 -3 = -3 -4 = -4 -5 = -5

SEX	RESP	'74	'75	'77	'82	'83	'85	'86	'88	'89
F	+5	42%	36%	38%	42%	36%	39%	42%	47%	39%
	+4	23	24	22	23	25	22	20	20	23
	+3	16	21	20	15	17	21	17	14	16
	+2	7	7	8	9	10	9	8	8	6
	+1	6	7	7	7	9	6	9	7	9
	-1	2	2	2	2	1	1	1	2	2
	-2	1	1	1	1	1	0	1	1	3
	-3	1	1	0	1	1	1	1	1	0
	-4	0	0	0	0	0	0	0	0	1
	-5	1	0	1	1	0	0	1	1	1
# SURVEYED		756	768	774	816	861	802	825	522	540

SEX	RESP	'74	'75	'77	'82	'83	'85	'86	'88	'89
M	+5	45%	40%	39%	45%	40%	43%	43%	44%	38%
	+4	23	24	24	23	23	24	23	21	21
	+3	13	17	17	16	21	17	16	15	19
	+2	8	10	9	8	8	9	9	9	8
	+1	7	6	6	5	5	4	6	9	7
	-1	1	2	2	1	1	1	1	1	2
	-2	1	0	1	1	1	0	0	0	1
	-3	1	1	1	0	0	1	0	1	0
	-4	0	0	0	0	0	1	0	0	0
	-5	1	0	0	1	1	0	1	1	2
# SURVEYED		670	648	662	627	671	667	611	424	417

☛ Both sexes agree that Canada's a great country to love: less than 2% separates the opinion of males and females.

☛ Canadaphiles beware: A comparison of the first two years of the survey with the last shows that the Canada's favorable ranking slipped from 81% to 79%.

Anglophiles R We

ENGLAND—A JOLLY GOOD PLACE?

What a difference 200 years makes. Had this survey been initiated in the 1770s instead of the 1970s, the results might have been quite different. Support for the British would have been at an all-time low, except in certain Tory communities. Now it's so much easier to like England, since, with the help of our therapists, we no longer fear being invaded by them. We also have our own native cuisine and several sporting events that help make us distinct. And we don't have a queen, unless you count the Nancy Reagan years.

Yes, we're not a country to carry a grudge about issues as slight as taxation without representation, redcoats (such good targets) invading our shores, tennis on grass courts, and the English interpretation of the American language.

England is second only to Canada in the affections of American women and men. In 1985 (the last year the question was asked), more than two-thirds (67%) ranked England +3 or higher.

Q: **On a scale that goes from "plus 5" for a country you like very much, to the lowest position of "minus 5" for a country you dislike very much, where would you rate England?** NOTE: 1972-1973, 1976, 1978-1981, 1984, 1986-1989.

SHE SAID HE SAID

Responses:	+5 = +5	+4 = +4	+3 = +3	+2 = +2	+1 = +1
	-1 = -1	-2 = -2	-3 = -3	-4 = -4	-5 = -5

SEX	RESP	'84	'85	'86	'87	'88	'89
F	+5	19%	18%	21%	22%	22%	19%
	+4	22	19	19	19	19	22
	+3	25	26	24	25	24	28
	+2	12	13	12	14	12	12
	+1	11	14	13	13	14	14
	-1	4	4	4	3	3	3
	-2	1	1	2	1	2	2
	-3	1	2	1	2	2	0
	-4	1	1	1	1	1	0
	-5	3	1	2	1	1	0
# SURVEYED		750	756	755	812	858	295

SEX	RESP	'84	'85	'86	'87	'88	'89
M	+5	16%	17%	18%	21%	21%	24%
	+4	19	15	18	20	21	19
	+3	26	26	22	23	22	23
	+2	17	15	15	14	15	17
	+1	11	14	15	12	13	10
	-1	5	4	5	3	3	2
	-2	2	2	3	2	2	1
	-3	2	3	1	2	2	2
	-4	1	1	1	0	0	1
	-5	3	2	2	2	2	1
# SURVEYED		669	644	651	625	670	417

☛ England rose in popularity after 1982, as Anglo-U.S. relationships improved and Republican presidents found a soulmate in Prime Minister Margaret (Iron Maggie) Thatcher.

☛ On average, women are 4% more likely to be Anglophiles. Among men, England's popularity fell to 58% in 1975-1977, but our boys gave their boys a symbolic slap on the back after the Falklands war — popularity among males rose 6% between 1977 and 1982. Among women, popularity rose 2% during the same period.

☛ Charley and Di make a cute couple, don't they?

Meet your new landlord: Mr. Osaka

JAPAN: SPLIT FEELINGS

We think they build high-ticket quality, so we buy a lot of their cars, TVs, cameras, bicycles, and stereos. And we're starting to buy $100 steaks from them as well, incredibly rich with fat (very good for the arteries) and culled from cows babied with beer (imagine the burping).

In return, they're proud to invest in the USA. While some feel this is akin to economic colonization, the Japanese believe that America represents a great land of opportunity (one of several they have worldwide). So they purchase our banks, golf courses, art, businesses, buildings, and media empires. Actually, they'll pretty much buy anything not nailed down. We've all played Monopoly with this sort; with a surplus of cash, they make no distinction between Baltic Ave. and Park Place. Money in hand, they say but one thing: "I'll buy it." Actually, what the Japanese seem to like most of all is real estate, since there's a lot less property to negotiate in Japan.

On the whole, we'd rather be bought by Canadians (31% to 9%), but our esteemed Northern Neighbors don't have the money (spending it all on cigarettes and season hockey tickets). Many Japanese (66% in a recent poll) think a lot of our economic problems are due to laziness, while we think they engage in unfair trade practices (61%). 77% of the Japanese think the reason that we have a trade imbalance is because Japanese products are better. We think they build a better product too; 91% of the 1,614 respondents to a 1990 *Cincinnati Enquirer* poll thought that Japanese products were average or above average in quality. And Japanese market share of the American automobile market has been steadily increasing for two decades.

So no lack of issues exists between us. Yet men and women are still very positive about Japan, rating it third behind

Canada and England. Men (Lee Iacocca was not questioned) in particular found favor with Japan. On average, men rated Japan a substantial 6% higher than women, although the male negative ranking of Japan picked up 2% between the first three and last three years of the survey (25 to 27%). Women actually showed a decline in their negative rating, moving from 32 to 28%.

The high regard that American men and women have for the Japanese work ethic and electronic wizardry is evident in the relatively high percentage of male (41%) and female (36%) respondents who ranked Japan in the top three categories over the last three survey years.

Yet both male and female opinion showed some ups and downs, driven by allegations of unfair trade practices and news of Japanese purchases of American turf. Thrown in for good measure is a dash of lingering prejudice, ironic in that the Japanese have been taking a lot of heat lately for alleged discriminatory practices aimed at blacks and the handicapped. A recent *Newsweek* poll of Japanese citizens found that 57% thought that one of America's serious problems was too many racial and ethnic groups.

Although Japan bashing is supposedly a popular pursuit, the country has gained esteem among female respondents and lost very modestly among males. For the first three survey years, the male approval rating in the top three categories averaged 42%, declining less than 1% during the last three years, an indication that men who thought well of Japan still felt that way. 33% of the female respondents rated Japan highly in 1974-77, an approval rating which increased to 36% in 1986-89. Within the moderate area (+1 and 2), female respondents increased 2% in the last three survey years, to 36%. Male moderates lost 2% during 1986-89, dropping to 32%, with those percentage points slipping into the negative rankings.

How do American men and women feel about Japan today? An April 1991 poll in *Business Week* found that 73% of the American public believes Japan got away without contributing its fair share to coalition forces in the gulf. 68% of the 1,255 adults queried would like a harder line on trade with Japan, and 64% say they are less likely to buy Japanese products. Only 28% admire Japan's economic success a great deal, down 21% from the same poll in 1989. 72% think that the economic threat from Japan poses a greater threat to the future of the country than the military threat from the Soviet Union.

And who do the Japanese pick as the next century's number one economic power? 42% pick the U.S., while 50% say Japan will be number one in the 21st Century, according to a 1990 *New York Times*/CBS News/Tokyo Broadcasting System poll.

Q: **On a scale that goes from "plus 5" for a country you like very much, to the lowest position of "minus 5" for a country you dislike very much, where would you rate Japan?**
NOTE: 1972-1973, 1976, 1978-1981, 1984, 1987.

Responses: +5 = +5   +4 = +4   +3 = +3   +2 = +2   +1 = +1
          -1 = -1   -2 = -2   -3 = -3   -4 = -4   -5 = -5

SEX	RESP	'74	'75	'77	'82	'83	'85	'86	'88	'89
F	+5	7%	5%	5%	7%	6%	8%	7%	8%	7%
	+4	11	8	7	9	7	10	10	8	9
	+3	19	17	20	21	16	19	20	20	20
	+2	16	15	14	14	16	16	17	15	13
	+1	18	21	19	19	21	19	19	21	22
	-1	8	10	11	10	11	9	9	10	9
	-2	5	5	5	5	7	5	6	4	5
	-3	6	7	6	6	7	7	4	6	5
	-4	5	6	6	3	4	3	3	1	2
	-5	5	5	7	6	5	4	5	7	8
# SURVEYED		739	750	748	800	853	789	806	513	544

SEX	RESP	'74	'75	'77	'82	'83	'85	'86	'88	'89
M	+5	9%	8%	10%	9%	8%	9%	10%	10%	8%
A	+4	10	12	7	11	9	11	11	10	12
L	+3	26	23	21	21	18	22	25	19	19
E	+2	15	15	15	15	18	18	17	14	13
	+1	18	18	20	15	19	15	15	19	18
	-1	6	8	7	8	10	9	6	9	8
	-2	4	5	5	5	4	5	5	5	7
	-3	3	4	6	4	6	5	4	4	4
	-4	3	3	3	4	3	2	1	3	2
	-5	7	5	7	8	6	3	5	8	9
# SURVEYED		667	638	651	623	668	664	609	421	418

☛ Which age group found the most disfavor with Japan? The 60+, with 39% ranking it at -1 or below for the last three survey years. Apparently, the last big one is still not over for some.

☛ 45% of the 30-35 group (demographically inclined toward Hondas) gave Japan a +3 or higher rating.

☛ For the last three survey years, 33% of the black respondents (369 surveyed) gave Japan a negative rating, compared to 28% of the white respondents (2,838 respondents).

☛ Other recent surveys show that positive opinions toward Japan are eroding. In 1990 a *New York Times* poll found that 25% of Americans had "generally unfriendly" feelings toward Japan, up from 8% in 1985, and 19% in 1989.

☛ In a 1990 poll published in *Fortune*, 61% of Americans felt that Japan unfairly restricts the sales of U.S. goods in Japan; 65% also feel that the U.S. should restrict Japanese imports.

☛ A 1990 poll by the Gallup Organization found that U.S. distrust of the Japanese was at its highest level in 30 years. This poll was commissioned by the Japanese Foreign Ministry.

☛ Japanese don't feel as positive about us either: 33% of the Japanese citizens surveyed by *Fortune* in 1990 said their respect for the U.S. had declined in the last five years. 11% said it had increased, and 56% had no opinion. 71% thought they made better televisions.

Women more sympathetic

ISRAEL:
IN SEARCH OF LOST POPULARITY

Israel has the dubious distinction of being the country, among those included in this survey, that lost the most favor with male and female survey respondents between 1974 and 1989. Comparing averages for the first three and last three survey years, the positive response (top five categories) by males declined from 71 to 58%. The drop among female respondents was nearly as steep: 70 to 61%. The average annual gender gap amounted to a substantial 6%. In the 1991 survey, that may reverse somewhat, given the restraint Israel displayed during the gulf war, the constant TV pictures of SCUD missile bombardments in Israeli neighborhoods, and recent reports indicating that Hussein was building super guns capable of shooting chemical payloads hundreds of miles (bringing Israel well within range).

Long considered an ally of the U.S. and an underdog in a hostile region, Israel has more recently been criticized for intransigence and human rights violations in the Palestinian uprising. Americans still solidly support Israel, but support may not be as deep as it once was. In a 1990 poll published in the *New York Times,* 61% of the respondents supported sustaining or increasing U.S. aid to Israel, while 47% support giving the Palestinians a homeland in the occupied territories of the West Bank and the Gaza Strip (a proposal that is opposed by the Israeli government). A recent *Newsweek* poll showed that 30% of Americans thought Israel had become a more important ally of the U.S. since the Iraqi invasion of Kuwait, while 52% felt that the Israel's role had not changed.

Q: **On a scale that goes from "plus 5" for a country you like very much, to the lowest position of "minus 5" for a country you dislike very much, where would you rate Israel?**
NOTE: 1972-1973, 1976, 1978-1981, 1984, 1987.

Responses:	+5 = +5	+4 = +4	+3 = +3	+2 = +2	+1 = +1
	-1 = -1	-2 = -2	-3 = -3	-4 = -4	-5 = -5

SEX	RESP	'74	'75	'77	'82	'83	'85	'86	'88	'89
F	+5	16%	10%	12%	12%	11%	13%	12%	11%	10%
	+4	9	8	11	9	9	9	10	7	6
	+3	16	15	16	15	10	16	12	12	12
	+2	12	13	12	12	12	14	13	9	11
	+1	19	20	20	16	19	16	20	18	20
	-1	9	12	11	13	13	11	10	13	11
	-2	5	6	7	7	7	7	6	7	7
	-3	5	5	5	5	7	6	6	9	6
	-4	3	4	3	4	5	3	5	3	5
	-5	6	6	4	6	6	5	6	11	12
# SURVEYED		730	742	733	779	833	768	794	500	506

SEX	RESP	'74	'75	'77	'82	'83	'85	'86	'88	'89
M	+5	13%	11%	14%	11%	9%	11%	12%	10%	9%
	+4	11	10	11	8	7	9	8	6	6
	+3	18	15	14	15	13	14	13	10	12
	+2	14	12	13	12	10	14	13	11	10
	+1	18	20	20	18	19	20	21	16	19
	-1	9	12	11	13	15	11	11	15	11
	-2	3	6	4	9	7	6	6	10	9
	-3	5	7	5	6	8	5	5	8	7
	-4	2	3	3	3	4	3	3	3	4
	-5	6	5	6	5	8	6	9	10	14
# SURVEYED		647	623	639	614	660	650	597	411	410

☛ Comparing the first three survey years to the last three years, the average female response in the top three categories declined from 38% to 31%, while the male response dropped a full 10% from 39%.

☛ Perhaps most telling is the number of respondents who described Israel as a country they "dislike very much" (a -5 rating). Over the survey's 16 years, this figure more than doubled, from 6% to 14% for men, and 6% to 12% for women.

☛ The youngest survey block was more negative about Israel than most: over the last three survey years, 22% of the 18-23 group rated Israel in the top three categories and 22% in the bottom three categories, with an overall 44% ranking Israel in the negative. The oldest group, in comparison, was slightly more positive, with 29% of the 66+ in the top three and 22% ranking Israel in the bottom three (43% negative overall).

☛ The 60-65 was one of the more divided, with 34% ranking Israel in the top three categories and an equally strong 25% ranking it in the bottom three (although the group had a moderate 36% negative total) the 36-41 was one of the more extreme pro-Israel blocks, with a league-leading 35% in the top three and a minimal 18% in the bottom three (37% across the negative board).

☛ Blacks and other minorities registered a 42% negative rating, averaged over the last three years of the survey (458 respondents). During the same period, white respondents gave Israel a 40% negative rating (2,760 surveyed).

But women are still suspicious

TO RUSSIA, WITH LOVE?

Did you know that: Russia is the biggest country on the globe, extending across 11 time zones?

That every three years or so, it has a new five-year rebuilding plan? (So that's where pro football coaches got the idea...)

That the latest trend toward liberalization is at least the third one since the death of Stalin? That 76% of 1,526 adults surveyed by *The Washington Post* think the world is a safer place due to the changes that have occurred in the Soviet Union and the Easter Bloc countries?

That Russia isn't the official name of the country may have contributed to its low performance to in the "favored country" series, but we suspect America's reasoning runs even deeper. Generally, both men and women's favor toward Russia hinged on news of our relations with the Soviet Union, which improved substantially during the Gorbachev years, but still has a way to go before a full thaw is reached. A 1990 survey published in *The Boston Globe* of 1,002 registered voters found that 44% of the men thought the Cold War was over, while 60% of the women did not. However, as a group we're much more worried about terrorism that a sudden attack by the Russians. 82% of that same 1990 Washington Post survey see terrorism as a greater threat to the U.S. than the military might of the Soviet Union.

Since Gorbachev took over the Soviet leadership in 1985, both women and men have found Russia more appealing and frankly sexier, although women less so than men. From 1985-89, male respondents have averaged 43% and females 38% in the top five categories, compared to 37% (male) and 33% (female) from 1974-83. Men may be more likely to see the Soviets as a big corporate account that has to be won over in order to ensure the world is safe for capitalism. Women are more likely to see the country in terms of human rights violations. Of course, we hate to generalize.

During the last three years of the survey, a mere 57% of the female and 51% of the male respondents felt negative about Russia, leading us to suspect that we are on the verge of the majority giving a positive grade to Russia. The survey respondent who puts Russia over the top will receive a week's vacation with some expenses paid on the Black Sea, sure to become a worldwide vacation mecca during the 21st century (you can be there first!).

Despite a hard-core anti-Russkie segment, a significant number of Americans have been more sympathetic. In 1974, 22% of males and 17% of females placed Russia in the top three ranks. In 1982 this ranking bottomed out at 6% and 5%, as President Reagan re-heated the cold war with Leonid Brezhnev and Yuri Andropov. Andropov and his successor, Constantin Chernenko, did little to pull the ratings out of the cellar, but things began to change when Gorby hit the scene running in 1985.

By 1989, with the world rapidly changing, Russia's favorable rating (21% for men and 19% for women) had nearly reached its 1974 level.

So what do we think of each other? In a 1990 *Los Angeles Times* poll, U.S. and Soviet citizens were asked their impression of each other as a people. Some 74% of 2,144 Americans polled rated Soviets favorably, while 86% of 1,485 Soviets we're positive about Americans. In a more recent (1990) poll published by the *Atlanta Journal and Constitution,* 41% of Americans said their attitudes toward the Soviet Union were "generally favorable," while 41% said "neutral." Only 14% said "unfavorable."

And now they have a McDonald's. We drink lots of their vodka. The world is a smaller place, *nyet?*

Q: **On a scale that goes from "plus 5" for a country you like very much, to the lowest position of "minus 5" for a country you dislike very much, where would you rate Russia?**
NOTE: 1972-1973, 1976, 1978-1981, 1984, 1987.

| Responses: | +5 = +5 | +4 = +4 | +3 = +3 | +2 = +2 | +1 = +1 |
| | -1 = -1 | -2 = -2 | -3 = -3 | -4 = -4 | -5 = -5 |

SEX	RESP	'74	'75	'77	'82	'83	'85	'86	'88	'89
F	+5	2%	2%	2%	1%	0%	2%	2%	3%	4%
	+4	3	2	2	1	1	1	1	2	3
	+3	12	12	9	5	4	4	7	9	12
	+2	11	11	7	4	5	4	6	11	12
	+1	16	19	12	11	12	12	15	19	21
	-1	13	12	14	10	12	10	13	11	10
	-2	6	5	5	5	8	6	7	6	8
	-3	10	10	9	10	14	12	11	10	7
	-4	4	6	6	6	8	7	7	4	4
	-5	24	22	33	45	37	41	30	25	18
# SURVEYED		745	749	761	819	861	793	802	515	535

SEX	RESP	'74	'75	'77	'82	'83	'85	'86	'88	'89
M	+5	4%	4%	2%	1%	1%	2%	1%	3%	4%
	+4	4	3	1	1	1	2	2	3	6
	+3	14	14	9	4	4	3	8	10	11
	+2	11	11	7	5	5	5	9	11	14
	+1	20	16	17	11	13	12	18	24	24
	-1	9	10	12	11	15	14	14	11	11
	-2	5	6	6	7	8	10	8	5	5
	-3	8	8	9	8	13	11	13	8	6
	-4	3	4	5	6	7	7	4	5	2
	-5	22	22	31	46	34	35	24	20	16
# SURVEYED		666	637	654	626	667	657	603	415	416

☛ In each year but one, the highest percentage of respondents ranked "Russia" -5, the lowest position possible. The extreme low point was reached in 1982, which was, curiously, a year before the Soviet Union shot down a Korean jetliner, killing all 269 passengers.

☛ Men have consistently given Russia higher marks than women, but not by much. The annual difference was 2%.

☛ The older the age group, the more negative toward Russia it was likely to be. 64% of the 66+ group rated Russia in the red, while only 44% of the 18-23 block turned thumbs down.

☛ A 1990 *Chicago Tribune* poll found that only 33% of Americans considered the Soviet Union a "serious threat."

☛ A 1990 *Detroit News and Free Press* telephone poll of 800 adults in Michigan on the popularity of George Bush and Mikhail Gorbachev resulted in both receiving the same job approval rating. 93% thought that the two leaders were doing a fair to excellent job.

Appearing on stage:
The comedy team of Marx & Lenin

MODERN COMMUNISM: IS THIS ANY WAY TO RUN A GOVERNMENT?

More men and women are describing communism as mere-ly "bad, but no worse than some others." Comparing the first three survey years with the last three, female respon-dents had a 4% increase in the "bad, but no worse" cate-gory, moving from 25 to 29%. Male responses jumped like-wise, growing from 29 to 35%.

To American men and women, the Soviet Union is the most obvious manifestation of the communist way, and opinions about communism have closely followed the peaks and valleys in U.S.-Soviet relations.

Known for its totalitarian ways during the cold war, The Soviet brand of communism recently suffered the embar-rassment of failing as an economic system too. The Soviet communists act much more like us these days: economi-cally bewildered, whining about costs, and looking for economic solutions. We've got the crack problem, they've got employees stoned on vodka. World domination is out of the question; they're having trouble enough just hang-ing on to their socialist republics and keeping the bread lines down. And of course, Gorby has become more pop-ular, winning Nobel prizes and scoring big numbers in U.S. popularity polls, although his own country is decid-edly ambivalent about him.

So where does this leave the anti-communist movement? After all, it's hard to look the villain straight in the eye if he's having trouble holding up his pants. Strident anti-communism has fallen off slightly since its peak in the early 1980s, when the Soviet Union shot down a Korean jetliner and confirmed for many women and men President Reagan's "evil empire" characterization. Overall, women have a significant edge in the anti-communist ranks: in the category, "worst kind of all," females averaged 55% for the last three survey years, compared to 46% of the males, both slight increases from the first three years (54% and 44%).

The "all right for some countries" category suffered a decline, with the female average dropping from 20 to 13% and the male from 24 to 17%. Nobody, it seems, wants to put up with those long lines for buying consumer goods.

Q: **Thinking about all the different kinds of governments in the world today, which of these statements comes closest to how you feel about Communism as a form of government?** NOTE: Question not asked in 1972, 1975, 1978, 1979, 1981, 1983, 1986.

Responses:　WS = It's the worst kind of all
　　　　　　BD = It's bad, but no worse than some others
　　　　　　AR = It's all right for some countries
　　　　　　GD = It's a good form of government

SEX RESP	'73	'74	'76	'77	'80	'82	'84	'85	'87	'88	'89
F WS	49%	55%	57%	58%	64%	65%	64%	64%	61%	52%	53%
BD	26	25	25	22	23	24	25	22	25	30	33
AR	24	18	17	19	12	10	10	12	13	15	12
GD	2	2	1	1	1	1	1	1	1	2	1
# SURVEYED	764	768	800	813	797	835	841	819	800	555	568
SEX RESP	**'73**	**'74**	**'76**	**'77**	**'80**	**'82**	**'84**	**'85**	**'87**	**'88**	**'89**
M WS	39%	45%	47%	48%	52%	55%	57%	52%	49%	45%	44%
BD	30	30	28	28	32	27	28	32	34	35	37
AR	26	21	24	22	15	15	12	14	15	18	18
GD	5	4	2	2	1	2	3	2	2	2	1
# SURVEYED	681	670	656	683	629	629	591	675	623	391	438

☛ In 1982 and 1984, 61% (56% male, 65% female) called communism "the worst form (of government) of all." But in the Gorbachev era of "peristroika" and "glastnos," this response declined to 49%.

☛ Women usually disapprove of communist forms of government more vehemently than men. Over the course of the survey, women described communism as "the worse kind of all" by an average of 10% more than men.

☛ Still fighting the cold war was the 60+ age group, with 61% declaring communism the worst government of all (last three years averaged).

☛ The 18-23 block fears no commies: 30% say it's bad, but no worse; 26% think it's all right for some (last three years).

☛ More philosophical but still opposed are the 30-35s: 39% think communism is bad, but no worse than others. Only 16% believe it's okay for some.

☛ 25% of the black respondents (last three years) thought communism okay for some, compared to 13% of the white respondents.

Your money or your life

IS THE WAR ON CRIME TOO EXPENSIVE?

Organized crime is big business, and its lesser version, disorganized crime, is a thriving small business. The guy on the street who holds you up likes to picture himself as a private entrepreneur trying to get ahead in life; the Mafia would rather you think of them as General Motors or AT&T, a well-established corporate icon filled with benevolent concern over the future of the human race. A war on crime, given the diversified fronts, could well turn out to be the mother of all domestic battles. But the general population is yearning to wage such an attack: for the 15 years of this survey, a strong majority of both women and men think we're spending too little to stop or at least slow down crime in America. The numbers vary little across the two decades: an average of 67% of the male and 73% of the female respondents believe that we're shortchanging our own safety (and sacrificing property) by not spending enough to combat crime.

Why might they feel this way? Well, for openers, crime statistics in America are staggering. Our homicide rate for men, 14 per 100,000 people (the majority of which are young black men), is nearly five times that of Canada. We are, hands down, the most violent industrialized nation in the world, and that's not even counting football Sundays. Violent crime, in particular against women, is up. 5% of violent crime occurs in *schools*. And the numbers keep climbing:1989 witnessed a 3% increase in overall crime, as did 1990. Our reputation is such that the Japanese, whose crime rate is rapidly escalating, term crime "the American disease." Nice of them to name something after us; in return we'll henceforth refer to karaoke as that "stupid Japanese social custom."

More astonishing than even that last paragraph is this: the

majority of major crimes are not even reported. Estimates are that official crime statistics are off by some 600%. Which sounds like a lot to us. After reading all that, you would expect great unanimity in the response category; who could be comfortable with the crime inflation rate that seems to be turning America into a *Road Warrior* sequel?

Yet with the enemy knocking down our doors, 25% of the male and 22% of the female respondents said our spending was just right (from 1987-89). 5% of the male and 4% of the female respondents said we were spending too much. Why? Were they members of the mob? Living with a lamp shade over their heads? Lifting the survey representative's wallet?

Perhaps spending on crime is a thornier issue than it appears. Location plays a role: crime surges are much more spectacular in the city than in the country. And, given our government's rather careless way with expenditures, we may not have the greatest of faith that money spent is money well spent. Just how do we use the extra resources to curb crime? Do we hire more police and build more prisons? Enact stricter penalties? More tightly impose the law while somehow maintaining the rights and freedoms of law-abiding citizens? How do we balance short-term goals (get the criminals off the streets) and long-term objectives (eliminate the social environment that breeds criminal behavior)?

Q: **We are faced with many problems in this country, none of which can be solved easily and inexpensively. I'm going to name some of these problems, and for each one I'd like you to tell me whether you think we are spending too much money, or about the right amount. Halting the rising crime rate.** NOTE: Question was not asked in 1972, 1979, 1981.

Responses: TL = Too little   AR = About right   TM = Too much

SEX	RESP	'73	'74	'75	'76	'77	'78	'80	'82	'83	'84	'85	'86	'87	'88	'89
F	TL	70%	72%	71%	72%	73%	69%	75%	77%	73%	75%	69%	71%	73%	73%	77%
	AR	27	23	25	20	23	26	20	19	23	22	27	25	23	23	20
	TM	3	5	4	8	5	5	6	4	4	3	4	4	5	4	3
# SURVEYED		732	741	762	774	774	841	785	809	855	241	306	405	244	398	418

SEX	RESP	'73	'74	'75	'76	'77	'78	'80	'82	'83	'84	'85	'86	'87	'88	'89
M	TL	68%	69%	68%	66%	67%	65%	68%	73%	66%	65%	63%	61%	69%	70%	72%
	AR	25	26	24	25	25	27	24	19	28	29	30	33	27	26	21
	TM	7	5	7	9	8	8	7	8	6	6	7	6	5	4	7
# SURVEYED		673	664	638	639	657	619	615	618	666	228	412	288	217	281	321

☛ Comparing the first three with the last three survey years, we find 2% more men and 3% more women chose the "too little" spending category.

☛ The average annual male/female opinion gap is 5%.

☛ Black respondents were strong advocates of increased spending, with 79% in the "too little" category over the last three survey years. White respondents averaged 72% during the same period.

☛ Age group most strongly advocating increased spending is the 60-65, with 80% saying "too little" during the last three survey years. Age group least supportive of increased spending is the 30-35, with 67% in the top spot.

Crime and punishment

IMPOSE THE DEATH PENALTY?

Crafty politicians know a popular issue when they see one. Take, for instance, the death penalty. Very few people seem to be against it. Generally, American women and men think that if you kill someone on purpose, than you should be executed. This is not punishment as a deterrent. Justice should be able to squeeze the hammer for its own sake, the people say. It's a tidy arrangement, disheveled only by reality, but more about that in a moment.

During the last three survey years, 81% of the male and 73% of the female respondents said they favor the death penalty. Men particularly like the idea of equal justice; in every survey year, an average of 10% more men than women favored the death penalty. Woman are more often accused of citing morality as a reason for opposing murder, whether accomplished by a madman or, that useful euphemism, the state.

But in spite of their differences today, men and women may be destined to meet in near-equal numbers on the death penalty issue at some date in the not-too-distant future. Averaging the first three and the last three survey years, 9% more men and 11% more women now favor the death penalty for murderers. Undoubtedly, some of this reflects our frustration with the rising crime rate and declining confidence in the judicial system. And incidents such at the Central Park wilding spree may lead people to believe that an ever-growing incorrigible criminal element exists that no judicial or penal system can hope to control.

So kill 'em.

The brutality of the age we live in certainly makes the "eye for an eye" philosophy more attractive. Mass homicides, the victims random, are frequent lead stories on the news. Men like Richard Speck and Charles Manson and the Son of Sam and John Gacy and Ted Bundy and John Humberty and Patrick Purdy and Jeffrey Dahmer become part of our twisted folklore. We, the people, have no hope of either understanding or reforming these individuals. We have no interest, either. Executing them could well be justice; more than 75% of the population believes it could live with the collective guilt. Remove these people from the planet Earth and let them rot in hell, we say.

But back to that slight problem we have with reality: rarely are homicide cases so open and shut. In the past, we've been somewhat haphazard about administering the death sentence fairly. And we've made a number of mistakes. Many studies suggest that black people are the recipients of death sentences far more than their percentages within general society, or even the criminal justice system, would dictate. Which may suggest their greater reluctance to support such a sentence. While 80% of the white respondents favored a death penalty during the last three survey years, only 52% of the black respondents did. And in July of 1991, the Supreme Court limited death row appeals to one trip through state and federal appeals, sharply reducing delays in executions. This is bad news for the 2,400 inmates currently on death row.

So what are our alternatives? In a 1990 survey, 80% of respondents in the state of California favored the existence of the death penalty. But when asked if a life sentence could be guaranteed, 67% of the respondents favored that option as opposed to the death penalty. 50% would give the death penalty to juveniles. 35% would execute mentally retarded individuals convicted of homicide.

A 1990 *L.A. Times survey* of 1,667 Californian residents provides some interesting tangents. While almost 80% of the respondents favor the death penalty, 31% feel that it is always morally wrong to take a life. 76% feel it is wrong to execute criminals as a money-saving tactic, and 70% asserted that revenge should not be a motive for capital punishment. Surprisingly, a full 80% felt that innocent people are sometimes executed, and 36% believe that minority groups are more apt to receive the death penalty than whites who commit the same kind of crime.

In Georgia, 64% favor the death penalty as the punishment for first degree murder, according to a 1990 survey of 652 adults in *The Atlanta Journal and Constitution.*

Q: **Do you favor or oppose the death penalty for persons convicted of** murder? NOTE: Question was not asked in 1972, 1973, 1979, 1981.

Responses: **FA = Favor**   **OP = Oppose**

SEX RESP	'73	'74	'75	'76	'77	'78	'80	'82	'83	'84	'86	'87	'88	'89
F FA	63%	59%	63%	67%	66%	66%	75%	72%	71%	77%	70%	72%	72%	74%
OP	37	41	37	33	34	34	25	28	29	23	30	28	28	26
# SURVEYED	736	754	780	757	818	759	804	864	807	789	797	761	769	811

SEX RESP	'73	'74	'75	'76	'77	'78	'80	'82	'83	'84	'86	'87	'88	'89
M FA	70%	71%	75%	77%	76%	78%	83%	84%	80%	83%	82%	77%	81%	84%
OP	30	29	25	23	24	22	17	16	20	17	18	23	19	16
# SURVEYED	668	629	646	666	625	613	614	659	569	662	593	605	604	636

☛ A significant shift in attitudes on the death penalty occurred during the '80s for both women and men. From 1974 to 1980, 75% of the male and 64% of the female respondents were in favor of the death penalty. During the conservative Reagan era, however, these percentages grew to 82% for men and 73% for women.

☛ Although black respondents are less supportive of the death penalty, they show an increased level of support for the proposal. Comparing the first with the last three survey years, 12% more favor execution.

☛ Among age groups, the 60-65 and 36-41 are slightly more in favor of the death penalty, with 79% over the last three survey years. Least supportive are the 18-23 and 54-59, with 70% in favor.

I have a gub and I know how to use it

DO YOU HAVE A GUN IN THE HOUSE?

Blessed is our right to keep and bear arms: 52% of the males surveyed had handguns in their home. 38% of the females did, averaged for the last three survey years. For the population as a whole, that's somewhere in the neighborhood of 75 to 100 million guns out there, in cabinets and tucked away in garages, some loaded, some not. The Wild West was never this dangerous.

Fewer women are now armed: figures for female respondents declined 5% from the early '70s mark of 43%. More than half the men surveyed are still well-armed, with no decline reported.

Gun ownership among female respondents peaked in 1977. Apparently the Carter presidency made them feel less secure. Men waited until Carter's last stand, 1980, before stocking up on firearms in anticipation of the Reagan years.

Other than the Brady Bill, anything worth noting about trends in gun ownership restrictions? A 1990 survey published in *Parents* revealed that 89% believe there should be a two-week waiting period between applying to buy and gun and taking it home. 75% would endorse a law outlawing semiautomatic weapons. 37% favor a law making it illegal to own or buy a handgun. 56% said widespread availability of handguns increased violent crime. 30% said gun ownership by private citizens helps preserve our country's freedoms.

87% of 600 gun owners surveyed for *Time*/CNN in 1989 favored a federal law requiring a seven-day waiting period and a background check for anyone wanting to buy a handgun.

A *Parade* magazine poll in 1990 of 140,000 readers revealed that 67% agreed that a 10-day waiting period should be required before a gun purchase. 65% said that a "ballistic fingerprint" should be filed on every weapon.

And how about those gun-toting Texans? A 1990 survey of 1,021 Texans, 52% of whom owned guns, discovered that 82% favored a seven-day waiting period to buy a handgun.

Q: **Do you happen to have in your home or garage any guns or revolvers?** NOTE: Question was not asked in 1972, 1975, 1978, 1979, 1981, 1983, 1986.

Responses: YES = Yes   NO = No   RF = Refused

SEX RESP	'73	'74	'76	'77	'80	'82	'84	'85	'87	'88	'89
F YES	43%	42%	43%	47%	41%	39%	40%	36%	43%	33%	39%
NO	57	58	56	53	58	60	60	63	57	66	61
RF	1	0	1	0	0	1	1	0	0	1	0
# SURVEYED	799	789	827	832	820	860	870	843	824	573	584

SEX RESP	'73	'74	'76	'77	'80	'82	'84	'85	'87	'88	'89
M YES	53%	51%	52%	55%	56%	54%	53%	54%	51%	50%	55%
NO	46	48	47	45	44	44	46	45	48	49	45
RF	1	1	1	0	0	2	1	1	1	1	0
# SURVEYED	696	690	666	689	637	638	596	687	640	397	446

☛ The average annual difference between men and women is 13%.

☛ White respondents are better armed than black: for the last three survey years, 47% of the white respondents reported they had a handgun in the house. Only 27% of the black respondents did.

☛ Age group most influenced by Schwarzenneger and Eastwood films is the 48-53, with 57% reporting that they owned handguns (last three survey years).

☛ Age group most susceptible to an ambush is the 24-29, with 32% owning a gun.

No, make him feel right at home

IS IT RIGHT TO FIGHT AN INTRUDER?

You may not have thought so, but it's safer on the subway than it is at home, although there's no standing in the aisle at home. In 1989, Americans were thirteen times more likely to be assaulted at home than on public transportation. Which may mean that we all need to just get out a little more. Neither women nor men take particularly well to the idea of being victimized in their own homes; they're mad as hell and not going to take it anymore.

Men were remarkably consistent in their response, with 88% (for the life of the survey) approving of whacking a stranger who had broken into the home. Women were slightly less approving during the 11 years of the survey, with 84% agreeing that beating a housebreaker was quite all right. Men, standing faithfully by their motto ("My home is my castle and whoever should have the sad misfortune of confusing it with a K-Mart at 4 a.m. shall suffer my wrath, just as soon as I find my slippers"), are more inclined than women to condone striking an intruder. The annual average difference between the sexes was 4%.

Women were also more likely to experience years of near pacifist restraint, such as 1984, when only 80% approved. Warrior males never did let down their guard.

Comparing the first and last three survey years, men were ever so slightly more inclined in the latter years of the survey to condone fisticuffs, while women were less so. From 1973-76, male respondents averaged 88% in the "hit 'em over the head" category (we paraphrase). From 1987-1989, a startling 1% increase occurred as George, Sidney, and Stanley, holdouts from the earlier survey period, said okay, let's fight. Female respondents averaged 86% during the first three and 84% during the last three survey years. Are women reacting to the question, which asks them to condone male aggression? Are women simply less inclined to condone violence in any context? And are all those who disapprove of striking an intruder pacifists, or do they resist on the grounds that fists might be met with fire?

Q: **Would you approve of an adult male punching a stranger if the stranger had broken into the man's house?** NOTE: Question was not asked in 1972, 1974, 1977, 1979, 1981, 1982, 1985.

Responses: YES NO

SEX RESP	'73	'74	'76	'77	'80	'82	'84	'85	'87	'88	'89
F YES	86%	90%	83%	83%	81%	82%	80%	85%	83%	83%	85%
NO	14	10	17	17	19	18	20	15	17	17	15
# SURVEYED	542	590	811	867	797	882	849	827	791	543	564

SEX RESP	'73	'74	'76	'77	'80	'82	'84	'85	'87	'88	'89
M YES	87%	92%	86%	86%	86%	88%	86%	88%	86%	90%	90%
NO	13	8	14	14	14	12	14	12	14	10	10
# SURVEYED	456	470	658	631	629	677	577	610	627	432	436

☛ The difference between men and women's opinion on the matter increased from 2% (based on an average of the first three years) to 5% (based on an average of the last three years).

☛ For the last three survey years, 86% of both black and white respondents were in complete agreement on fighting the intruder.

☛ Fighting an intruder in the home cut across age lines as an issue: the age groups all approved to very near the same degree.

Wait until dark

AFRAID IN YOUR OWN NEIGHBORHOOD?

That women are considerably more fearful than men to walk alone at night is no revelation (even though males are far more apt to be the victims of violent crimes committed by a stranger). But "considerably" hardly describes the situation: women are more than three times as anxious about a stroll in the dark. For the last three survey years, female respondents who said they were worried about solitary nocturnal walks in their own neighborhoods averaged 56%. Only 18% of the male respondents were uneasy.

What is baffling is the trend in recent years among both men and women to be less afraid to walk alone at night; even more baffling is that women outstrip men in their decreased anxiety about wandering away from the homestead after dark. This decrease is in spite of the usual grim statistics: 22% of American women and 37% of American men will be robbed at some point in their lives...and burglary is even more common than robbery. What's more, 60% of Americans have been victims of a major crime, and of those, 58% have been victimized twice.

Women are still plenty worried, but less so than they were a decade ago. From 1973-82, 62% of the female respondents said they were fearful of walking in the local area at night. From 1984-89, that percentage dipped to 56%, and shows indications of further decline. Strangely enough, the male response changes during the same time period: from '73 to '82, males answering "yes" averaged 23%, and thereafter only 19%. For reasons unknown and in spite of statistics, somewhere around 1983 or '84, women and men became more secure in their own neighborhoods.

Q : **Is there any area right around here—that is, within a mile—where you would be afraid to walk alone at night?** NOTE: Question was not asked in 1972, 1975, 1978, 1979, 1981, 1983, 1986.

Responses: YES   NO

SEX RESP	'73	'74	'76	'77	'80	'82	'84	'85	'87	'88	'89
F YES	60%	63%	61%	63%	61%	61%	58%	56%	56%	57%	55%
NO	40	37	39	37	39	39	42	44	44	43	45
# SURVEYED	792	784	826	832	817	863	855	833	819	569	584

SEX RESP	'73	'74	'76	'77	'80	'82	'84	'85	'87	'88	'89
M YES	20%	24%	23%	23%	21%	28%	19%	21%	17%	17%	19%
NO	80	76	77	77	79	72	81	79	83	83	81
# SURVEYED	696	688	666	688	639	639	596	685	638	397	443

☛ Comparing the average of the first three with the last three survey years, both women and men experienced a 5% decrease in neighborhood anxiety after sunset.

☛ Black respondents had more reservations about walking after dark in their own neighborhoods: for the last three years of the survey, 54% of the black respondents said yes, they were worried. 38% of the white respondents agreed.

☛ Vulnerability goes with age: the three most anxious age groups over the last three survey years were the 54-59, with 42% in the "yes" column; the 60-65, with 51%; and the 66+, with 50%. In comparison, the 18-23 averaged 39%, the 24-29, 41%, and 30-35, 34%.

SEX
& DRUGS

In which we find women to be more discriminating

MALE SEX PARTNERS SINCE AGE 18

And the shocking conclusions to our survey: in comparison with men, women, by and large and perhaps generally as well, have had fewer sexual partners of the opposite sex. 88% of the females polled have had six or fewer male sexual partners, compared to 62% of the males with females. The percentage includes 7% who have not had a male sex partner, as compared to 5% of the men who had not had a female sex companion.

The incidence of homosexual partnering is roughly the same for both sexes, although women again have had fewer sexual partners. At the upper levels of the sex-o-rama (25 partners or more), women are virtual nonparticipants when compared to the male stats.

What does this prove? That both heterosexual and homosexual women have less need for multiple sex partners and are less likely to engage in casual sex? Perhaps. That women are more discriminating in their choice of sexual partners? Maybe. That women may not be quite so forthright about their sexual activity? A possibility. Though on all the surveys dealing with sex, women rarely match the sexual numerical levels attained by men. For women, the consequences of casual liaisons with the opposite sex can be dramatic: pregnancy. And while both sexes must ponder the possibility of AIDS, women may be taking the threat more seriously.

Q : **Now thinking about the time since your 18th (including the past 12 months) birthday, how many male partners have you had sex with?**
NOTE: Question was not asked in 1972-1988.

Responses:

0 = 0	1 = 1	2 = 2
3 = 3	4 = 4 - 6	5 = 7 - 9
6 = 10 - 14	7 = 15 - 24	8 = 25 - 997

Year	Sex	Resp	
'89	F	0	7%
		1	43
		2	13
		3	10
		4	15
		5	3
		6	4
		7	3
		8	2
# SURVEYED			716

Year	Sex	Resp	
'89	M	0	93%
		1	2
		2	1
		3	1
		4	1
		5	0
		6	0
		7	0
		8	1
# SURVEYED			563

☛ 88% of the women surveyed have had six or fewer male sex partners since age 18. 63% of the females had two or less male sex partners; 38% counted two to six partners; 12% claimed more than six partners; 7% had 15 or more. 6% could remember the exact location of their elementary school and 33% admitted that they occasionally ran stop signs, particularly while driving.

☛ On the Female Sex Partners Since Age 18 table, no female claimed more than 4-6 female partners (1%). On the other hand, male sex partnering with other males had a 1% lodged in the 25-997 category.

Men and women count, sometimes using more than one hand

FEMALE SEX PARTNERS SINCE AGE 18

Perhaps the most revealing stat is that the majority of men questioned have had six or less female sex partners since the age of 18, although statistically men do appear to have more sex partners of the opposite sex than females, by a significant margin. The incidence of homosexuality is relatively even, with the incidence of female to female sex numerically equivalent to male to male sex, although it involves different anatomical parts. And that the spawning period of the spotted trout, rare in most fresh waters outside the Missoloupi in upper Volta, is less than 12 minutes annually, ensuring that foreplay remains a matter of philosophy rather than practice.

Q: **Now thinking about the time since your 18th (including the past 12 months) birthday, how many female partners have you had sex with?**
NOTE: Question was not asked in 1972-1988.

Responses:
0 = 0   1 = 1   2 = 2
3 = 3   4 = 4 - 6   5 = 7 - 9
6 = 10 - 14   7 = 15 - 2   8 = 25 - 997

Year	Sex	Resp	
'89	F	0	94%
		1	2
		2	1
		3	1
		4	1
		5	0
		6	0
		7	0
		8	0
# SURVEYED			690

Year	Sex	Resp	
'89	M	0	5%
		1	21
		2	6
		3	9
		4	21
		5	4
		6	9
		7	11
		8	1
# SURVEYED			540

☞ 62% of American males report having had six or fewer female sex partners since they were 18 years old. 43% report that they still have their first baseball glove.

☞ 5% of the males have had no female sex partners. On the female side of the ledger, 5% report having had sex with other women, about the same as males with males.

☞ Some 33% of the men questioned have had between 10 and 997 female partners since the age of 18. To narrow it down further, some 20% have had between 10 and 24 partners, while 13% claim more than 24 and less than 1,000. 3% say they have found big money in the folds and corners of car seats.

Just the truth, the whole truth

HOW FREQUENTLY DO YOU HAVE SEX?

Good news, bad news. First the bad news: a fair number of people, some of whom you may know, do not or seldom have sex, at least in the characteristic mode of enjoying it with another person. The good news is that many men and women are sexually active at least once a week, with a significant portion of the survey respondents enjoying sex two to three times a week.

A recent study by the National Opinion Research Center found that married people had sex an average of 67 times per year. Separated people checked in at 66 attempts annually, and divorced people at 55.

When compared to the male survey responses, more than twice as many women have elected to just say no to sex; while we don't know the reasons, we suspect it has something to do with men and/or sex. And perhaps television as well.

Respondents' age also had a lot to do with frequency. In the 66+ group, 64% were not having sex while 12% enjoyed close encounters one to three times a week (231 surveyed). The 30 to 35s seemed out to set new land speed records for sexual activity, with 63% claiming to have sex at least once a week (192 surveyed). And those newly embarked on the bumpy journey to independent adulthood, the 18 to 23s (129) reported 21% not having sex, a mark which declined to 7% for the next age group, the 24 to 29s (187).

Q: **About how often did you have sex during the last six months?**

SHE SAID HE SAID

Year	Sex	Resp		Year	Sex	Resp	
'89	F	NO	29%	'89	M	NO	13%
		YR	8			YR	7
		MN	8			MN	9
		23	16			23	17
		WK	16			WK	23
		2W	20			2W	26
		3+	4			3+	5
# SURVEYED			777	# SURVEYED			584

☛ How much shall we allow for the culturally induced modesty of women and braggadocio (perhaps also culturally induced) nature of men in these matters?

☛ Some readers seem surprised that people are having sex so *seldom*. Others are surprised at how *often* people are having sex. The first group seems to have an exaggerated estimation of others' sexual prowess compared to their own. The second group is surprised that so many others are as obsessed with sex as they are.

☛ Sexual inadequacies abound. Researchers, armed with more information and sophisticated statistical methods, can make much of these responses. The rest of us would do well to take these self-reported statistics with a grain of salt, fun as they are.

TV or not TV?

WHERE DOES THE TELEVISION SET RATE IN YOUR LIFE?

Despite the presence of greater numbers of women in the workforce than ever before, more women than men reserve the time for heavy exposure to the boob tube (four or more hours a day). The average annual difference between males and females watching mucho TV is more than 9 points. Averaging the last three years of the survey, 36% of the women possess a heavy television dependency, while 27% of the male survey audience qualify as certified couch potatoes. The Frequency of Sex poll discovered that twice as many women as men were not having sex; with all this television watching, where would they find the time? Of course, you can watch lots of television and still have lots of sex. It's just harder to pay attention.

Although the survey indicates no precipitous drop in viewership for either sex, a 1990 *USA Today* survey of 2,000 people found that 70% of the respondents claimed to be watching less television than they were a year ago. Certainly they are watching less network television, as ratings will attest. The survey also found that 78% have cable, 58% thought television too predictable, 40% said it was too violent and 28% said that TV fare is too racy, while 8% felt it to be entirely too tame. An infinitely small number claimed not to understand how to operate a set and that if man was meant to fly, God would have given us all commuter jets.

Q: **On the average day, about how many hours do you personally watch television?** NOTE: Question was not asked in 1972-1974, 1976, 1979, 1981, 1984, 1987.

Responses: 0 = 0 Hours   1 = 1   2 = 2   3 = 3   4 = 4
5 = 5 - 6   6 = 7 - 8   7 = 9 - 10   8 = 11 - 12
9 = 13 or more

SEX	RESP	'75	'77	'78	'80	'82	'83	'85	'86	'88	'89
F	0	4%	4%	5%	6%	5%	6%	5%	4%	3%	4%
	1	15	18	19	17	20	17	16	17	18	18
	2	25	23	26	23	23	25	24	25	22	28
	3	20	21	19	19	18	20	19	20	19	14
	4	15	16	13	13	15	13	15	13	15	16
	5	14	12	12	16	11	13	16	13	16	12
	6	3	4	3	3	4	3	4	4	4	5
	7	2	1	1	2	2	1	1	2	2	1
	8	1	1	1	1	1	1	0	1	1	1
	9	0	1	1	1	1	1	1	1	1	1
# SURVEYED		815	835	885	817	866	906	838	846	544	570

SEX	RESP	'75	'77	'78	'80	'82	'83	'85	'86	'88	'89
M	0	3%	4%	7%	9%	4%	5%	5%	5%	3%	3%
	1	20	24	23	20	22	20	20	19	20	19
	2	29	28	29	26	27	26	28	28	29	33
	3	19	20	19	19	21	21	22	21	20	20
	4	14	10	12	14	12	13	12	13	13	12
	5	11	10	8	9	10	11	8	8	11	10
	6	2	2	2	3	2	3	2	3	2	2
	7	0	1	0	0	0	1	1	1	1	1
	8	1	0	0	0	1	0	0	1	1	1
	9	0	0	0	0	0	0	1	1	1	0
# SURVEYED		668	690	643	637	638	689	685	620	435	428

☛ Between 1975-1978 and 1986-1989, the survey experiences a modest increase in the number of people heavily exposed to TV — about 3% more men and women. Cable and home videos may well have contributed to this slight swell in committed couch potatoville.

☛ Among age groups, television viewing remains fairly steady, averaging 20 to 25% in the heavy viewing category, for groups up to the age of 54. From that point on, heavy viewing tends to escalate, ranging in the 30 to 50% range, with the 66 and up crowd most enjoying televised entertainment and news (49% watching four or more hours per day in 1989—169 surveyed).

☛ Nearly 2,000 readers of *USA Weekend* (of 4,700 who responded to a survey) said that they wouldn't want to live next door to the Bundys of Fox's *Married With Children*.

Men say they have sex more often with virtual strangers

SEX WITH A CASUAL DATE

It should come as no surprise that men, more than women, claim to have sex far more frequently with people they just sort of run into. Sex roles and expectations being what they are, men are inclined to be sexual opportunists and measure success on a date more highly if it culminates in sex or results in a set of free automobile shock absorbers. And given their impulsive "I am lion of my suburb and lord of all the local fast food and video establishments" demeanor, sex with somebody they don't even know may not strike them as unwise or unusual. Until later.

Of course, we're in the last decade of the 20th century and killer sexual diseases are a big story and casual sex flies in the face of correct sexual politics, proving perhaps that an overdose of testosterone may subdue the senses and leave one particularly defenseless while in the sway of a certain sashay. Did ye get lucky?

Q: **Was one of your sex partners in the last 12 months a casual date or pickup?** NOTE: Question was not asked in 1972-1987.

Responses: YES NO

Sex	Resp	'88	'89
F	YES	15%	10%
	NO	85	90
# SURVEYED		65	60

Sex	Resp	'88	'89
M	YES	36%	36%
	NO	64	64
# SURVEYED		105	100

☛ Compared to females, males reported more than twice the percentage of sexual encounters with a casual date or pickup in a twelve-month period.

214

☛ Voted most likely to engage in casual sex is the 24 to 29 year-old age group, with an average of 37% just saying yes for the two years of the survey (87 questioned).

☛ The annual average male/female difference is 23.5 percentage points, over the two survey years in which this question has been asked. Men show no reduction in their rate of casual sex from 1988 to 1989, while women report a decrease of 5%.

☛ Hypothetical rhetorical device: if casual sex is not safe sex (who's to say?), how do we account for male disregard of widely distributed information on AIDS and other sexually transmitted diseases. Perhaps it is native male stupidity, an exaggeration (oh ya, I scored, sure), or perhaps they thought the question was, "Was one of your dates at the miniature golf course a casual one?"

☛ The sample size is small and not enough data has been collected to track any trends, predict sex group or group sex behaviors, or be of any help in selecting lottery numbers.

If you can't be with the one you love...

SEX WITH A PROPER ACQUAINTANCE

Side by side they work together, sharing occupational hazards and successes, each secretly fantasizing about the other. "I wonder what he looks like in bib overalls," she ponders. "Does she have all her teeth?" he muses. And then one day she looks hotly at him and he looks dreamily at her and then they both look vacantly out the window, temporarily diverted by faraway foghorns bellowing on the lake or the echo of honking geese on the marsh or the distant whistle of a lonesome locomotive thundering through a long dark passage. "Listen to those ducks," he whispers, but it's not to the muted bleats of supposed wildlife she's concentrating on anymore. "Those are foghorns," she breathes.

Or perhaps they live next to each other, engaging in harmless suburban flirting while pulling weeds from the lawn or rolling the garbage bins down to the curb or while washing the car. And they fantasize. "What does she look like in one of those business suits with the funny ties?" he wonders. "He seems so nice; I bet he knows how to change an electric fuse," she thinks. And then one day he looks hotly at her and she returns his gaze just before a twin-seater glider crash lands 20 yards away. But after a glance at the wreckage their eyes meet, the same desire dancing the mambo between them...

Or maybe they've known each other a long time, perhaps not very well, but in an amiable, slightly suggestive way that always seemed on the verge of meaning something. And then one day she finds herself in his arms and he looks at her and she looks at him and suddenly a big wave crashes on the beach conveniently placed before them, but they pay no attention...

Cinematic fantasy or reality? The interesting point is that so many chose their sex partners from people they see on an everyday basis. The office or workplace are fabled to be a hotbeds of sexual intrigue and neighbors have been known to be quite friendly and long-term acquaintances can be trusted, at least some of the time. And it's, oh, so convenient.

Q: **Was one of your sex partners in the last 12 months a neighbor, co-worker, or a long-term acquaintance?** NOTE: Question was not asked in 1972-1987.

Responses: **YES NO**

Sex	Resp	'88	'89	Sex	Resp	'88	'89
F	YES	32%	37%	M	YES	34%	30%
	NO	68	63		NO	66	70
# SURVEYED		65	60	# SURVEYED		105	100

☛ In 1989, female respondents led the way, trysting the night away with familiars some 7% more than males.

☛ The 24-29 age group, the largest segment of the survey population in 1989 with 42 members, answered yes 48% of the time.

Or how to become closer to your close friends

SEX WITH A CLOSE FRIEND

The majority of both men and women surveyed say that, yes, they have had sex with a close personal friend in the last year. Which may mean that men and women, those two sides of the same coin, are more likely to have sex with people familiar and with whom they share a trust, particularly in this age of AIDS and other sexually transmitted diseases. And many times within a relationship, the best friend may well be the significant other. So we asked that question, too, and the answer is below.

Of course, we did not define "best friend" and the question only asked if "one" of the sex partners was close. Which could mean that the other 43 were total strangers. But the answer to the survey leads us to suspect that real intimacy is still alive and well in America, but perhaps living under an assumed name.

Q 1: **Was one of your sex partners in the last 12 months a close personal friend?** NOTE: Question was not asked in 1972-1987.

Responses: YES NO

Sex	Resp	'88	'89
F	YES	66%	73%
	NO	34	27
# SURVEYED		65	60

Sex	Resp	'88	'89
M	YES	65%	67%
	NO	35	33
# SURVEYED		105	100

Q2: Was one of your sex partners in the last 12 months your husband or wife or regular sex partner? NOTE: Question was not asked in 1972-1987.

Responses: YES NO

Sex	Resp	'88	'89
F	YES	94%	93%
	NO	6	7
# SURVEYED		562	569

Sex	Resp	'88	'89
M	YES	89%	90%
	NO	11	10
# SURVEYED		499	509

☞ Although the sexes are quite equal in their preference for combining sex with deep friendship, women are slightly more inclined to have sex with soul mates. This trend is consistent with the other sexual behavior surveys shown here, with women supportive of fewer and deeper relationships.

Not looking for love in all the wrong places

CLOSE ENCOUNTERS OF THE EXTRAMARITAL KIND

Men and women uniformly believe extramarital sex is wrong, indicating that reverence for marital vows remains high despite soaring divorce rates. Since 1973, the percentage of men opposing extramarital affairs has grown from 64% to 75%; women from 74% to a high of 83% in 1988. As with most questions of sexual morality, women exhibit a distinctly more rigorous attitude toward the upholding of traditional mores.

The curious state of affairs with this survey is that those who believe that extramarital sex is always wrong are a growing majority, in spite of the so-called sexual revolution and abundant evidence that infidelity occurs with regular frequency. Some experts estimate that one-third to one-half of married persons have cheated on their spouses. Tom W. Smith, director of the General Social Survey from which this book was derived, observes the difference between behavior and belief. "About three quarters (of respondents) have always said it's wrong," he says. "But that doesn't mean infidelity isn't occurring."

On the other hand, some polls suggest that most men and women are not playing around behind the back of their spouses. A poll based on telephone interviews with 657 adults in 1989 found that fewer than 1 in 10 currently married people admitted having been unfaithful. A 1990 survey of 815 men from age 18 through retirement discovered that the respondents thought that marital fidelity was equally important for the man (79%) and the woman (82%). 88% would marry their wives again.

Q: **What is your opinion about a married person having sexual relations with someone other than the marriage partner—is it always wrong, almost always wrong, wrong only sometimes, or not wrong at all?** NOTE: Question was not asked in 1972, 1975, 1978, 1979, 1981, 1983, 1986.

Responses: AW = Always wrong   AA = Almost always wrong
               WS = Wrong only sometimes   NW = Not wrong at all

SEX RESP		'73	'74	'76	'77	'80	'82	'84	'85	'87	'88	'89
F	AW	74%	78%	72%	77%	73%	76%	75%	77%	77%	83%	80%
	AA	14	10	14	13	15	13	18	14	14	12	11
	WS	9	9	10	8	9	9	6	7	7	5	8
	NW	2	2	4	2	3	3	1	2	2	1	1
# SURVEYED		801	780	813	827	811	855	861	836	816	569	579

SEX RESP		'73	'74	'76	'77	'80	'82	'84	'85	'87	'88	'89
M	AW	64%	69%	64%	69%	67%	70%	65%	72%	70%	74%	75%
	AA	16	14	18	15	17	15	19	14	18	15	16
	WS	14	15	13	13	12	12	13	10	9	7	7
	NW	6	3	5	4	5	3	4	4	3	4	2
# SURVEYED		690	680	662	683	633	623	588	676	628	394	440

☛ A very large majority of the population, male and female, categorically condemn extramarital sexual activity. In fact, when the average of the first three years is compared with the average of the last three years we find that in the last three years 7% more men chose "Always wrong" and 5% more women chose that category. As a result, the initially wide gap between men and women on this issue (10% in 1973) has narrowed to a mere 5% by 1989. The average annual male/female difference is 7.5%

☛ Since the AIDS epidemic a new and very sobering dimension has been added to the morality of extramarital sex. The transgression of cheating on one's spouse is much more serious when it involves potentially exposing the spouse to a fatal disease as well as winking at the marriage vows.

☛ One of the age groups most opposed to extramarital sex is ironically the youngest and likely the least married—the 18-to-23 year-old, with 81% (of 97 surveyed) answering that extramarital sex is always wrong. They were exceeded only by the 48 to infinity group, with an average 84% (of 433 surveyed) answering no, no, no. Age groups representing the cutting edge included the 24 to 29s and 36 to 41s, with 15% believing that extramarital sex was either okay or mostly okay.

First you say yes then you say no

PREMARITAL SEXUAL RELATIONS

Given the revolution in morals that originated with the 60's rebellion, one would think that men and women's attitude toward premarital sex would show some telling changes. And indeed, there is a firm trend toward more permissiveness, with men showing greater enthusiasm (what a surprise) for sex before marriage. Women who believe that premarital sex is always wrong are decreasing in number, but still maintain a 10% edge over men in that survey category.

Men, on the other hand, hold the same edge in the category, "not wrong at all."

The majority of men and women believe that, at least some of the time, premarital sex is okay. For the last three years of the survey, women (and men) who meant maybe averaged 23%.

Since the early 70s, the opposition to premarital sex has gradually declined in number. Still, a significant number of men and women oppose premarital sex under any circumstances.

Q: **Television, movies, and news media often reflect a change in the way women and men perceive morals and attitudes toward sex. If a man and woman have sex relations before marriage, do you think it is always wrong, almost always wrong, wrong only sometimes, or not wrong at all?** NOTE: Question not asked in 1973, 1976, 1979-1981, 1984, 1987.

Responses: AW = Always wrong AA = Almost always wrong
WS = Wrong only sometimes NW = Not wrong at all

SEX RESP	'72	'74	'75	'77	'78	'82	'83	'85	'86	'88	'89
F AW	44%	36%	35%	37%	34%	32%	31%	34%	33%	29%	32%
AA	12	14	14	10	12	10	11	8	9	13	10
WS	24	25	24	22	20	21	24	19	23	24	22
NW	20	26	27	30	34	36	33	39	35	35	36
# SURVEYED	759	767	786	813	869	841	889	815	816	533	555

SEX RESP	'72	'74	'75	'77	'78	'82	'83	'85	'86	'88	'89
M AW	30%	30%	26%	24%	23%	23%	22%	22%	20%	23%	22%
AA	11	12	10	8	12	8	8	8	9	8	7
WS	24	22	24	24	20	21	25	21	23	21	24
NW	35	37	40	44	45	47	45	49	48	48	46
# SURVEYED	778	662	641	668	625	614	672	667	609	422	416

☛ Opponents of premarital sexual relations, at a 1972 high of 30% for males and 44% of females, have represented a minority of survey respondents from the first survey year to the present. But they are a committed minority, holding fast to their views from year to year and changing very slowly. In fact, the drop in opposition to premarital sex between earliest years (1972-1975) and latest ones (1986-1989) is the same for males and females —a relatively small, but notable 7%.

☛ The *average* annual male/female difference is a substantial 10%.

☛ Among age groups, the 30-to-35 year-old segment (followed closely by the 24 to 29s) is the most permissive (in 1989), with 60% believing that premarital sex is never wrong and another 23% feeling that it is only occasionally wrong (out of 140 surveyed). The jump from 1972 to 1989 was an astounding 29%! The 60+ age group was the most opposed to premarital frolicking, with more than 55% holding that it is always wrong (of 224 surveyed). Interestingly enough, the 60-65 year-old group actually showed an increase of 9% from 1972 who think that premarital sex is always wrong. Only one other group showed an increase between the first and last years of the survey in that category, the 18-to-23 year-old (from 11% to 18%).

☛ Responses to other questions involving sex (pornography, frequency of sex, X-rated movies, and so on) also show wide differences between men and women.

A hotbed of dissent

TEENAGE SEXUAL RELATIONS

A primary fear of parents, second perhaps only to contemplation that their children may never move out, is that their offspring will somehow sabotage their lives during the wild and crazy teen years. A major concern in the "it's my life" round of adolescent contention is sexuality. And it seems obvious after looking at the table below that most men and women do not view teenage sexual conduct ambivalently: it's always or almost always wrong, wrong, wrong. Adults would seem to view those adolescent years as the great fog era, where mature judgement and emotions are at odds with a teen psychology befuddled by the hormonal pursuit of youthful abandon.

Adolescents, on the other hand, have a much different perspective or at least behave distinct from what they believe. As part of a recent survey of condom usage and teenagers' knowledge of AIDS conducted at 26 randomly selected high schools in Indiana, 40% of the 2,300 teens involved admitted having intercourse. The youngest age group of our survey, the 18 to 23s, are more lenient about teen sex: for the three years of the survey, they averaged 46% always wrong, 24% almost always wrong, 24% sometimes wrong, and 6% never wrong (284 total surveyed).

Q: **For teenagers, say 14 to 16 years old, do you think sex relations before marriage are always wrong, almost always wrong, wrong sometimes, or not wrong at all?** NOTE: Question not asked in 1972-1985, 1987

Responses: AW = Always wrong   AA = Almost always wrong
                  WS = Wrong sometimes   NW = Not wrong at all

SEX	RESP	'86	'88	'89
F	AW	71%	73%	76%
	AA	19	14	13
	WS	9	10	7
	NW	2	2	4
# SURVEYED		838	542	571

SEX	RESP	'86	'88	'89
M	AW	61%	64%	64%
	AA	19	19	20
	WS	14	12	12
	NW	5	5	4
# SURVEYED		607	431	420

☛ The "Always wrong" category is the most popular with both male and female respondents asked about teenage sexual relations. Women in particular are apt to be sensitive about this issue, perhaps because they see more clearly the damage that a teen pregnancy can do to a young life. In all three survey years, women lead men by 9 to 12%. And with a net increase of 5% in three years, clearly their tendency is to become more conservative on this issue. The annual average sex difference is 10%.

☛ With the threat imposed by AIDS, people have become and are still becoming more negative toward teenage sex. Where moral reasons for abstinence leave off, now ethical and health reasons take over. The results of a 1990 survey of 1,200 Philadelphia teens found that 96% of the males and 94% of the females were more selective of sexual partners because of AIDS. 12% had stopped having sex.

Most women and men think not

IS HOMOSEXUALITY OK?

The great majority of women and men consistently oppose the idea of homosexuality, with a similarly consistent minority of some 21% who believe that it is not (or is only occasionally) wrong. The AIDS epidemic certainly has not made it easier for men and women to accept homosexuality, as suggested by comparing the responses for the first and last three years of the survey. For the first three years, an average of 77% of both men and women believe that homosexual acts are always or almost always wrong. For the last three years, the average response in the same categories is 80%.

On the other hand, the increasing openness and militancy of homosexuals in the workplace and elsewhere may be creating a better informed heterosexual majority that is no more tolerant. A poll published in *American Demographics* of March 1990 queried 30 to 49 year-olds about the lasting effects of the sixties generation. 59% agreed that greater tolerance of homosexuality as an alternative lifestyle was a negative change. Within our survey, 75% of the 30-47 age group felt that homosexual relationships were always or almost always wrong, averaged over the last three years of the survey.

Q: **What about sexual relations between two adults of the same sex—do you think it is always wrong, almost always wrong, wrong only sometimes, or not wrong at all?** NOTE: Question was not asked in 1972, 1975, 1978, 1979, 1981, 1983, 1986.

Responses: AW = Always wrong   AA = Almost always wrong
WS = Wrong sometimes   NW = Not wrong at all   OT = Other

SEX	RESP	'73	'74	'76	'77	'80	'82	'84	'85	'87	'88	'89
F	AW	74%	69%	71%	73%	74%	71%	74%	75%	77%	76%	73%
	AA	6	5	6	5	6	4	5	4	5	5	4
	WS	7	9	7	8	7	8	8	7	6	6	6
	NW	10	13	17	14	14	16	13	14	12	13	17
	OT	2	4	0	0	0	0	0	0	0	0	0
# SURVEYED		767	754	781	794	782	826	830	819	796	549	552

SEX	RESP	'73	'74	'76	'77	'80	'82	'84	'85	'87	'88	'89
M	AW	72%	72%	69%	70%	73%	76%	72%	75%	77%	78%	75%
	AA	7	5	7	6	6	6	5	4	3	4	4
	WS	8	7	9	7	5	4	7	7	7	5	6
	NW	12	13	15	16	16	13	16	14	12	12	14
	OT	2	3	0	0	0	0	0	0	0	0	0
# SURVEYED		681	658	645	659	615	609	582	665	616	388	428

☛ Men and women do not differ greatly in their opinions about homosexuality. The average annual male/female difference is 2%.

☛ The only noteworthy change is a trend in recent years for larger percentage of both sexes to view homosexuality as "Always wrong." When the average of the first three survey years is compared to the average of the three most recent survey years, 6% more men and 4% more women have joined the "Always wrong" category.

☛ Undoubtedly much of this negative change is fallout from the AIDS epidemic, which struck the homosexual community first and hardest. Since a high point in 1987 and 1988 of 76-77% for women and 77-78% for men, however, the ranks of homophobic respondents have again dropped to 75% for men and 73% for women.

☛ An average of 22% of the female respondents and 20% of the male believe that homosexual acts are seldom or never wrong.

☛ The age group least likely to condemn homosexual acts is 30 to 41 year-olds. During the last three years of the survey (904 surveyed), an average of 27% think such acts are not wrong or only occasionally wrong. Voted most likely to condemn is the 48 and over crowd, averaging 87% who think it always or almost always wrong during the same period (1,335 surveyed).

Should distribution be narrowed or broadened?

PORNOGRAPHY AND THE LAW

Pornography, whatever it might be (you know it when you see it), is still not something lightly debated between the sexes. The majority of men interviewed thought that the distribution of pornography should be limited to people over the age of 18. Among women, it's almost an even split between those who believe that laws should be enacted against the distribution of pornography, whatever the age of the reader/viewer, and those that would limit it to persons over 18.

The most liberal male segment that supports the unhindered distribution of pornography is gradually but significantly thinning, from an average of more than 11% during the first three years of the survey to just 6% during the last three years.

What does it mean? That the pro-pornography part of the population is losing its bang? That pornography as an experience is lacking in socially redeemable qualities? That there are better hobbies?

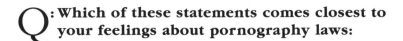

Q: Which of these statements comes closest to your feelings about pornography laws:

1: There should be laws against the distribution of pornography whatever the age;

2: There should be laws against the distribution of pornography to persons under 18;

3: There should be no laws forbidding the distribution of pornography. NOTE: Question was not asked in 1972, 1974, 1977, 1979, 1981, 1982, 1985.

Responses:
1 = There should be laws against the distribution of pornography whatever the age
2 = There should be laws against the distribution of pornography to persons under 18
3 = There should be no laws forbidding the distribution of pornography

SEX	RESP	'73	'75	'76	'78	'80	'83	'84	'86	'87	'88	'89
F	1	48%	46%	48%	51%	49%	50%	49%	52%	51%	52%	49%
	2	43	44	45	44	46	46	49	45	46	44	47
	3	9	9	6	5	5	4	3	4	3	4	3
# SURVEYED		786	813	808	878	805	893	853	843	815	546	581

SEX	RESP	'73	'74	'76	'77	'80	'82	'84	'85	'87	'88	'89
M	1	36%	34%	32%	34%	32%	31%	30%	31%	26%	34%	30%
	2	54	53	58	56	61	64	63	65	69	60	64
	3	10	13	11	10	8	5	7	4	5	6	7
# SURVEYED		683	658	657	637	631	681	593	612	629	429	437

☛ Women remain resolute about pornography. When the average of the first three years is compared with the average of the last three years we find that 4% fewer men chose category one and 3% more women chose that category. In every year more women than men chose to stop the sale of pornography to anyone. The average annual male/female difference is an incredible 18%, and the gap is widening from 12% in 1973 to 19% in 1989.

☛ Men who joined the opposition to selling pornography to children or adolescents came from both the more-liberal and the more-restrictive camps, since responses #1 and #3 decline as #2 (distribution to 18-or-under should be illegal) increases. Women joining the opposition to all pornography (response #1) and pornography for children or adolescents (response #2) came from the most liberal camp (response #3), which declined by the net amount of 6% from 1973 to 1989. Clearly women are becoming more restrictive on this issue, while men from both extremes of opinion are becoming more moderate.

☛ The age segment represented by respondents 48 and older was most opposed to any distribution of pornography, with an average of 58% against it for the last three years of the survey (1,343 respondents). No age group stands out as particular advocates of unlimited distribution; the group most favoring limited distribution, with scores in the +60% range, is the 18 to 41.

For sure it won't teach you a thing about auto mechanics

PORNOGRAPHY A SOURCE FOR SEX ED?

The majority of men and women surveyed believe that pornography supplies information about sex. The statement is more strongly supported by men than women, with an average of more than 64% of men responding "yes" in the last three years of the survey. In comparison, women said yes an average of 61% during the last three years. Of course, the question does not ascertain the quality of that information, good or bad, so the answers are only specific to the word "information." And while the majority of men and women agree that pornography does contain information about sex, it is a bit like saying that cookbooks have information on cooking, even if a particular book contains a lot of recipes that you don't want to try.

The age group most inclined to look upon pornography as sexually enlightening is the youngest. The 18 to 23 segment averaged 74% yes responses during the last three years of the survey (304 surveyed). When respondents are analyzed by race, white respondents averaged 61% yes for the last three years (2,772 surveyed); black respondents averaged 74% (382 surveyed).

Q: **Do sexually graphic materials provide information about sex?** NOTE: Question was not asked in 1972, 1974, 1977, 1979, 1981, 1982, 1985.

SEX ▼ DRUGS

Responses: YES   NO

SEX	RESP	'73	'75	'76	'78	'80	'83	'84	'86	'87	'88	'89
F	YES	65%	68%	59%	64%	63%	61%	60%	59%	65%	61%	58%
	NO	35	32	41	36	37	39	40	41	35	39	42
# SURVEYED		753	732	748	825	750	847	808	795	760	512	552

SEX	RESP	'73	'75	'76	'78	'80	'83	'84	'86	'87	'88	'89
M	YES	66%	68%	63%	67%	63%	66%	62%	62%	67%	64%	62%
	NO	34	32	37	33	37	34	38	38	33	36	38
# SURVEYED		663	627	640	612	608	665	581	596	610	418	426

☛ The sexes do not differ radically on this question. In all survey years a majority of both sexes agree that pornography provides some type of sex education. Men tend to take a 1 to 5 point lead on this issue, except in 1975 and 1980, when the sexes finished in a dead heat. The average annual difference between men and women was 2%.

☛ Also it should be noted that support for the "Yes" category has eroded over time. When the average of the first three years is compared with the average of the last three years, we find that 1% fewer men and 3% fewer women chose to say yes.

Electrical and otherwise

PORNOGRAPHY PROVIDES OUTLET?

Although the survey indicates a growing number of "yes" responses, it is not entirely clear what those votes mean. It may be that respondents interpret "provides outlet" to mean "allows people to get rid of bottled-up sexual feelings in a safe way" — a positive opinion of pornography. Another possible interpretation is that respondents take the phrase to mean "stirs up deep-seated sexual feelings in an undesirable or dangerous manner," so that the respondents selecting "yes" are actually taking a negative stance toward pornography. Then again, some may interpret "bottled up" as referring to the drain pipes under the sink, which have been clogged for quite a while now.

Given the high female percentages agreeing that **Pornography Incites Rape** (74% in 1989), a safe assumption is that many of the "Yes" votes here from females signify *disapproval* of pornography. In other words, when women say yes here, they mean no, and many of the "No" are disapproving as well, although some no's may actually be yes's, and vice versa. This particular survey may shed no new light on bottled-up impulses, but offers an entertaining debate along the lines of the "which came first, mind or matter?" issue that has befuddled philosophers and cab drivers for ages.

Q : **Do sexually graphic materials provide an outlet for bottled-up impulses?** NOTE: Question was not asked in 1972, 1974, 1977, 1979, 1981, 1982, 1985.

SEX ▼ DRUGS

SEX	RESP	'73	'75	'76	'78	'80	'83	'84	'86	'87	'88	'89
F	YES	61%	69%	66%	68%	68%	66%	70%	65%	71%	65%	72%
	NO	39	31	34	32	32	34	30	35	29	35	28
# SURVEYED		717	672	674	748	678	778	746	750	698	473	488

SEX	RESP	'73	'75	'76	'78	'80	'83	'84	'86	'87	'88	'89
M	YES	60%	65%	65%	66%	70%	63%	68%	67%	68%	64%	67%
	NO	40	35	35	34	30	37	32	33	32	36	34
# SURVEYED		631	577	582	596	580	634	540	567	571	387	400

☛ Regarding the previous question, Pornography Provides Sex Education, men took the lead in affirmative responses. But women are more likely than men to answer "Yes" to Pornography Provides Outlet, in all but two survey years (1970 and 1967).

☛ The group of respondents answering "Yes" to pornography provides outlet gradually is gaining ascendancy. When the average of the first three years is compared to the average of the last three years, men have increased "Yes" responses by 3% and women by 4%. The average annual male/female split on this issue is 2%.

Women say yes; men maybe
DOES PORNOGRAPHY INCITE RAPE?

Few surveys within this book show such a profound difference of opinion as this one. Women's anxiety about pornography must certainly be fueled by the increase in sex crimes against women that has taken place during the life (1972 to present) of the General Social Survey from which this data is taken. Potentially victims (according to an article in the *Washington Post* in December 1990, one in four women will be raped), women are not inclined to support any social subsystem that condones, supports, or popularizes the crime.

Much more so than women, men display a consistent ambivalence about making a direct connection between rape and pornography, with roughly half saying yes and half no. Men, although sharing concern about violence against women, are not threatened with it and are more inclined to associate this question with the need to safeguard free speech and freedom of the press. Men are likely also to be much more familiar with pornographic materials, with frequent exposure creating both a desensitized view of the material and a more individual awareness of the sexual dynamics involved. And it's hard to underestimate that recurring human philosophy: when you're not a victim, it ain't a crime.

Q: **Do sexually graphic materials lead people to commit rape?** NOTE: Question was not asked in 1972, 1974, 1977, 1979, 1981, 1982, 1985.

Responses: YES NO

SEX RESP	'73	'75	'76	'78	'80	'83	'84	'86	'87	'88	'89
F YES	61%	65%	65%	67%	66%	66%	67%	66%	67%	69%	74%
NO	39	35	35	33	34	34	33	34	33	31	26
# SURVEYED	737	717	743	806	737	832	788	782	748	511	542

SEX RESP	'73	'75	'76	'78	'80	'83	'84	'86	'87	'88	'89
M YES	46%	50%	50%	53%	51%	51%	49%	54%	50%	51%	52%
NO	54	50	50	47	49	49	51	46	50	49	48
# SURVEYED	653	618	613	610	591	644	560	578	580	398	413

☛ As usual with the pornography issue, wide disagreement between the sexes exists. In 1973, 46% of men and 61% of women believed that pornography incites rape. By 1989 that difference had grown to 22%. The average annual male/female difference is 16%.

☛ Although both men and women have become increasingly convinced that pornography incites rape, men change opinion much more slowly. Between the beginning and the most recent three survey years, men linking pornography to rape increased by 2%, while women increased by 6% on this issue over the same time span. As a result, men in 1989 were still 9% shy of the 61% level for women in 1973.

☛ Interesting split between the generations: for the last three years of the survey, the age group 18 to 41 averaged only a 52% yes response (1,601 surveyed). The age group 42 to eternity averaged a 70% yes response (1,581 surveyed), led by the 81% yes vote of the 66+ crowd (554).

M so blue looking at U

X-RATED MOVIE VIEWING

More men than women have watched X-rated movies in every year since this question was first asked in the survey. The annual average gap between men and women on this question is a hefty 11%.

Men likely watch more porn films because generally, the movies exploit male sex fantasies (no kidding?) and hold much less appeal for women. And women consistently show a more adverse attitude toward pornography throughout the sexuality surveys.

In the early 1970s, better-made sex films (at least comparatively) such as *Deep Throat* and *Behind the Green Door* created an aura of stardom for porn queens like Linda Lovelace and captured a larger audience in the process. VCR viewing obviously sparked the revival of blue movies during the 80s, an interest which now may well have peaked (after you've seen 10 X-rated movies, you've seen them all).

According to a poll of 657 married adults in 1989, 21% of married folks say they watch X-rated videos as a couple at least sometimes.

Q: **Have you seen an X-rated movie in the last year?** NOTE: Question was not asked in 1972, 1974, 1977, 1979, 1981, 1982, 1985.

SEX ▼ DRUGS

SEX	RESP	'73	'75	'76	'78	'80	'83	'84	'86	'87	'88	'89
F	YES	20%	15%	12%	11%	13%	15%	19%	20%	22%	20%	17%
	NO	80	85	88	89	87	85	81	80	78	80	83
# SURVEYED		800	815	827	884	823	905	868	843	819	556	583

SEX	RESP	'73	'75	'76	'78	'80	'83	'84	'86	'87	'88	'89
M	YES	31%	24%	26%	20%	20%	25%	30%	31%	35%	35%	31%
	NO	69	76	74	80	80	75	70	69	65	65	69
# SURVEYED		691	667	665	640	639	683	596	617	637	436	443

☛ In 1975 "Blue movies" went into a decline that hit bottom at the end of the 1970s. VCRs sparked a resurgence of interest in X-rated films, which peaked in 1987 for both males and females.

☛ From 1973-1976 to 1987-1988, X-rated movie viewing increased by 7% among males and 3% among females. It remains to be seen whether the 4-point decline in viewers in 1989 is a normal annual variation or the beginning of a new declining trend in viewership.

☛ During the last three years of the survey, the age group most enthusiastic about X-rated movie viewing is the 18 to 23s (surprise!), averaging a 47% hormonal *yes I watch X-rated movies* response (311 total surveyed). Least voyeuristic are the 66 and up group, sporting an overwhelming 95% no way, baby, I'd rather go fishing (622 total surveyed).

Norm!

SPENDING QUALITY TIME IN THE TAVERN

At most, only 25% to 33% of men and women respondents have been in the habit of frequenting bars. And the real curiosity is how many men and women *never* step into a bistro. The age group with the smallest numbers crossing the thresholds of local lounges is the 48 and up segment, which in 1989 averaged 72% who neither set foot nor lip in a taproom, while the 24-to-35 year-old group spends the greatest amount of time grinning in the gin mills, averaging 23% who visit on at least a weekly basis.

The survey indicates that bars hit their peak of popularity during the middle-and-late seventies' disco era, as they became a mecca of chic sociality and platform shoes. Fraternizing at the saloon remained relatively popular until the early and mid-eighties, when everyone was too busy making money during the Reagan Illusion. At that time, a visit to a local watering hole lost some of its glitter for both men and women, as perhaps health and related concerns became more dominant. Men – at 31%, their peak of patronage, in 1977 – still enjoy a visit to the pub more than women do, with a few diehards (2% in 1989) occupying their favorite stools on a near continual basis. Using the top three categories ("Almost Every Day," "Once or Twice a Week" and "Several Times a Month"), the average annual gender gap on this question is 15%.

Q : **How often do you go to a bar or tavern?**
NOTE: Question was not asked in 1972, 1973, 1976, 1979-1981, 1984, 1987.

Responses: DL = Almost every day   WL = Once or twice a week
SM = Several times a month   ML = About once a month
SY = Several times a year   YL = About once a year
NV = Never

SEX	RESP	'74	'75	'77	'78	'82	'83	'85	'86	'88	'89
F	DL	1%	0%	1%	1%	0%	1%	1%	0%	0%	0%
	WL	4	4	4	6	7	6	5	5	5	5
	SM	4	5	6	7	6	7	6	4	6	3
	ML	8	8	9	7	8	8	11	8	9	8
	SY	13	9	11	12	11	10	12	11	11	10
	YL	8	9	10	11	11	10	11	11	12	12
	NV	62	64	59	57	57	58	55	61	58	62
# SURVEYED		780	810	835	888	863	906	842	845	548	576

SEX	RESP	'74	'75	'77	'78	'82	'83	'85	'86	'88	'89
M	DL	4%	3%	5%	4%	3%	3%	3%	2%	2%	2%
	WL	16	12	15	12	15	15	12	12	12	12
	SM	8	9	11	12	7	11	11	8	8	8
	ML	11	10	11	8	10	8	11	12	11	10
	SY	12	9	11	13	14	13	11	13	11	11
	YL	7	10	9	9	11	11	10	9	14	10
	NV	43	47	39	42	40	40	42	43	43	47
# SURVEYED		682	666	690	640	632	687	687	618	435	428

☛ More men than women have lost interest in bars in the later survey years. Male bar patronage dropped by 6% between 1974-1977 and 1986-1989. Although women had a four-year stretch of relatively high patronage (with an all-time high of 14% in 1978 and 1983), by 1986-1989 their patronage had dropped slightly below the 1974-1977 level.

☛ Two major factors probably contribute to this decline: a vigorous federal anti-alcohol and drug campaign; and the waning attractiveness of casual sexual encounters with the onset of the AIDS epidemic.

A hard habit to break

GOING UP IN SMOKE

Smokers are a dying breed in this country. Although some of the non-smokers counted in the question "Current Smoking Habit" never took up the "weed" in the first place, many others are former smokers who succeeded in quitting.

"Attempted to Quit Smoking" was asked only of current smokers, a decision we believe was very wise; so "Yes" represents strictly the backsliders. Since this is true, it is not too surprising that the unsuccessful "quit" rate is not very different for one sex than for the other. The annual average difference between the sexes is 4%. It is encouraging to note that comparing the first three survey years with the last three, a greater percentage of each sex tried to quit smoking: 2% more for men, and 5% more for women. Maybe the next time they try to quit, they'll make it.

Q 1: **If you do not smoke now, have you ever smoked regularly?** NOTE: Question was not asked in 1972-1977, 1979, 1981, 1982, 1985.

Responses: YES   NO

SEX	RESP	'78	'80	'83	'84	'86	'87	'88	'89
F	YES	25%	25%	25%	22%	24%	29%	27%	30%
	NO	75	75	75	78	76	71	73	70
# SURVEYED		543	526	599	580	581	572	357	389

SEX	RESP	'78	'80	'83	'84	'86	'87	'88	'89
M	YES	49%	51%	45%	46%	44%	43%	42%	45%
	NO	51	49	55	54	56	57	58	55
# SURVEYED		330	324	397	328	368	392	251	278

Q 2: **Do you now smoke cigarettes?** NOTE: Asked only of current smokers. Question not asked in 1972-1976, 1979, 1981, 1982, 1985-1989.

Responses: **YES   NO**

SEX	RESP	'77	'78	'80	'83	'84
F	YES	99%	99%	99%	100%	99%
	NO	1	1	1	0	1
# SURVEYED		286	305	287	303	279

SEX	RESP	'77	'78	'80	'83	'84
M	YES	85%	83%	87%	91%	91%
	NO	15	17	13	9	9
# SURVEYED		352	293	307	286	262

Q 3: **Have you ever tried to give up smoking?** NOTE: Asked only of current smokers. Question was not asked in 1972-1977, 1979, 1981, 1982, 1985.

Responses: **YES   NO**

SEX	RESP	'78	'80	'83	'84	'86	'87	'88	'89
F	YES	68%	65%	75%	76%	71%	73%	79%	71%
	NO	32	35	25	24	29	27	21	29
# SURVEYED		305	290	303	279	242	223	170	167

SEX	RESP	'78	'80	'83	'84	'86	'87	'88	'89
M	YES	70%	72%	75%	72%	74%	68%	77%	79%
	NO	30	28	25	28	26	32	23	21
# SURVEYED		294	305	288	262	232	229	166	141

☛ The full array of data on the **Current Smoking Habit** question includes a breakdown by race, showing that the vast majority of whites (71% in 1989) have abandoned smoking. With this traditional market gone, tobacco companies have been accused of targeting advertising appeals toward teens, blacks, and citizens of countries less-sophisticated about the health hazards of smoking.

☛ Minorities (blacks at 40% and "other" at only 21% smoking in 1989) have slightly more smokers than whites; but they too have well under half of their respective populations smoking.

SHE SAID 🙂 🙂 HE SAID

Are $ spent too little, too much, too late?

DEALING WITH DRUG ADDICTION

Men and women have mixed feelings about spending public funds for drug problems. Some of the confusion stems from the solution most often proffered by the federal government: punishment of the perpetrators without addressing the economic and social conditions that create a seemingly endless supply of perpetrators.

A recent related survey published in the *Washington Post* measured the responses of 1,400 adults on two points: the Bush administration's policy of "more prison sentences for casual drug use, the use of the military...and more tax dollars spent on prisons" or making drugs legally available to adults while "providing more drug treatment and better education." The poll found 36% supporting the legalization/education option.

And what about the GSS poll? In the last four survey years (1986-1989), positive responses from men for increased spending have jumped from the lowest to the highest level ever. Women have been more temperate in their opinions. Female support for increased spending is the same in 1989 as it was in 1973 (and overall averages nearly 65%), while male support gained 7%. Support for increased spending among men peaks at 77% in 1989 (drawing most heavily from the "about right" segment) and dips to 56% in 1978 and 1986 (with increased spenders escaping to "about right"), a spread of 21%. The difference in the female response was a much more modest 11%.

Other related surveys: The 22nd annual Gallup/Phi Delta Kappa poll of the public's attitude's toward the public schools found that 76% thought it unlikely or highly unlikely that President Bush would attain his goal of making every school in America free of drugs and violence by the year 2000. A 1990 poll taken by the Weekly Reader, the school news publication, of 100,000 fourth and sixth graders discovered that 73% of the fourth graders see a need for drug and alcohol education, up from 57% in 1985.

Q: **We are faced with many problems in this country, none of which can be solved easily and inexpensively. I'm going to name some of these problems, and for each one I'd like you to tell me whether you think we are spending too much money, or about the right amount:**

Dealing with drug addiction. NOTE: Question was not asked in 1972, 1979, 1981.

Responses: TL = Too little   AR = About right   TM = Too much

SEX	RESP	'73	'74	'75	'76	'77	'78	'80	'82	'83	'84	'85	'86	'87	'88	'89
F	TL	71%	62%	60%	62%	61%	60%	66%	62%	63%	67%	65%	64%	69%	69%	71%
	AR	24	31	33	31	32	32	26	31	32	29	32	30	27	28	23
	TM	5	7	7	7	8	8	8	7	5	5	3	6	4	3	6
# SURVEYED		736	737	738	756	760	828	760	788	849	240	304	401	250	405	418
SEX	RESP	'73	'74	'75	'76	'77	'78	'80	'82	'83	'84	'85	'86	'87	'88	'89
M	TL	70%	65%	60%	64%	58%	56%	63%	61%	63%	64%	64%	56%	64%	73%	77%
	AR	23	28	29	26	31	33	28	28	30	28	28	36	32	22	16
	TM	8	7	12	10	11	11	9	12	7	7	8	7	5	5	8
# SURVEYED		663	659	632	634	650	624	593	599	658	227	411	294	221	286	318

☛ Male/female differences are not very significant; and the splits in male/female opinion do not demonstrate a consistently higher level of support among either males or females. The average annual gender gap on this issue is only 3%. For the life of the survey, women average nearly 65% and men 64% in favor of increased spending.

In God we often trust, but churches, well...

CONFIDENCE IN ORGANIZED RELIGION

Religious belief and confidence in organized religion are two distinct items. While our survey shows no significant changes in intensity of religious belief, confidence in organized religion seems to rank right up there with faith in politicians these days, with both men and women casting an equally jaded eye.

Back in '73, 35% of males and 37% of females professed "a great deal" of confidence in organized religion, but by 1989, these figures declined to 22% and 23%, respectively. The number of individuals with "hardly any" confidence in organized religion nearly doubled over the same time period, with 35% of the men and 28% of the women surveyed in 1989 indicating that they'd just as soon trust the brahmin of the religion business as a used car salesman.

Was public opinion affected by Jimmy Swaggart's 1988 scandal and Jim Baker's 1989 conviction? Do people really expect morality from their religious leaders? And has the ongoing confusion of church leaders (for instance, Protestants and sexual behavior—an oxymoron?) created insecurity among the masses?

Q: **I am going to name some institutions in this country. As far as the people running these institutions are concerned, would you say you have a great deal of confidence, only some confidence, or hardly any confidence at all in them? How much confidence do you have in the people running organized religion in this country?** NOTE: Question was not asked in 1972, 1979, 1981, 1985.

Responses: GD = A great deal   SM = Only some   HA= Hardly

SEX RESP	'73	'74	'75	'76	'77	'78	'80	'82	'83	'84	'86	'87	'88	'89
F GD	37%	47%	28%	32%	43%	33%	38%	35%	31%	33%	27%	32%	20%	23%
SM	48	44	52	49	47	49	43	50	52	48	51	50	51	49
HA	15	9	20	19	10	18	18	15	17	18	21	18	28	28
# SURVEYED	762	771	757	777	808	844	792	829	870	544	819	801	545	564

SEX RESP	'73	'74	'75	'76	'77	'78	'80	'82	'83	'84	'86	'87	'88	'89
M GD	35%	43%	24%	33%	39%	31%	35%	31%	27%	31%	24%	27%	21%	22%
SM	46	43	51	46	47	49	47	53	53	48	54	52	43	43
HA	18	13	26	20	14	20	19	16	20	21	22	21	36	35
# SURVEYED	680	679	633	620	667	624	617	624	662	401	598	615	422	431

☛ Comparing the average of the first three years with the last three years, we find that fewer men and women are expressing high confidence in religious organizations: an 11% decrease for men and a 12% decrease for women.

☛ The only split between the genders of any size at all was the 5% difference in 1987. The average annual gap between men and women is less than 3%.

☛ Among age groups, the 66+ lost much confidence but still led the other groups. 34% expressed "a great deal" of confidence in 1989 and 34% was the average for the last three years of the survey. In comparison, the seniors had an average of 45% during the first three years of the survey.

☛ In 1975, confidence in religious organizations eroded across the board: male and female, racial groups, and all age groups. President Nixon was gone, gas prices were up, the Vietnam War officially ended, and New York City dallied with default. In baseball, Cincinnati edged Boston in seven games, with Pete ("Lucky") Rose named MVP. But why the dip?

Perhaps let's do lunch, instead?

SEE YOU IN CHURCH?

Although many of the major religions complain of dwindling church attendance (a recent Gallup survey found that 78 million Americans do not belong to a church or synagogue or attend only on infrequent special occasions, up from 61 million in 1978), our survey indicates a certain consistency since the mid-1970s. True, fewer members of both sexes attended services with some regularity during the last three survey years than in the first three (averaging SY, OM, TM, NW, WK, and NW): males declined from 61% to 58%; females, the most ardent churchgoers, from 72% to 71%. And true, those that never attend church have increased in number between the first and last segments of the survey period: females from 10% to 13% and males from 14% to 18%.

But the minor point spread aside, nothing significant seems to be going on, other than females still attend church far more than males. Throughout the surveys, women seem more inclined than men to religious fervor. The average annual male/female difference across the 16 survey years is an astounding 12%.

What accounts for the constant gender discrepancy? Are men and women drawn to church for different reasons? Do the social and familial aspects of churchgoing play the same roles in men's as in women's church attendance? Does football get in the way? Do men go to church to meet women (obviously a lot of single ones are attending)?

Q: **How often do you attend religious services?**

Responses:
- NV = Never
- OY = About once or twice a year
- OM = About once a month
- NW = Nearly every week
- SW = Several times a week
- LY = Less than once a year
- SY = Several time a year
- TM = 2-3 times a month
- WK = Every week

SEX	RESP	'72	'73	'74	'75	'76	'77	'78	'80	'82	'83	'84	'85	'86	'87	'88	'89
F	NV	8%	13%	10%	12%	13%	12%	14%	9%	12%	12%	10%	13%	12%	11%	14%	14%
	LY	7	6	5	6	7	7	7	6	5	7	6	7	7	5	6	6
	OY	9	10	14	11	11	11	11	13	14	11	9	13	10	12	10	12
	SY	12	14	13	14	15	10	11	14	13	12	14	11	11	16	14	13
	OM	6	6	9	7	6	7	7	6	7	5	7	7	8	7	8	7
	TM	9	9	9	10	7	11	11	9	10	11	9	8	10	12	10	9
	NW	6	8	6	8	5	7	8	6	7	5	5	4	5	5	9	6
	WK	33	24	25	26	25	26	23	26	23	27	28	28	26	23	21	25
	SW	8	10	9	7	10	9	9	10	9	11	12	9	11	9	9	9
# SURVEYED		800	798	791	818	827	835	888	821	864	907	866	843	846	818	842	875

SEX	RESP	'72	'73	'74	'75	'76	'77	'78	'80	'82	'83	'84	'85	'86	'87	'88	'89
M	NV	11%	15%	15%	18%	13%	16%	18%	14%	18%	16%	17%	16%	17%	13%	22%	19%
	LY	10	9	9	9	11	10	11	10	10	9	9	7	8	8	9	9
	OY	13	16	17	14	17	16	16	19	17	16	16	18	16	17	13	15
	SY	16	16	12	14	16	15	12	17	15	12	15	14	14	16	12	12
	OM	7	6	6	7	9	8	7	7	6	8	8	8	8	10	7	9
	TM	8	8	8	8	7	7	8	7	6	9	7	7	10	8	9	7
	NW	6	7	6	5	7	4	5	6	5	6	4	4	4	5	6	4
	WK	24	17	20	18	14	16	15	16	16	18	18	21	18	17	16	20
	SW	5	5	7	6	7	8	7	5	7	6	6	6	6	5	6	5
# SURVEYED		800	697	690	669	665	686	639	640	631	688	594	687	620	636	636	658

☛ Although the average annual difference between men and women is 12%, it was 11% in the first three survey years and returned to 11% again in the last three, on average.

☛ Significantly more women than men attend church on a weekly basis. For the life of the survey, women averaged 26%, while men averaged only 18%.

☛ Despite the decline in church attendance, Americans are still lining the pews in far greater numbers than our European counterparts. As a matter of fact, more of us attend church in a week than attend all sports events combined.

Welcome to the Protestant Nation

RELIGIOUS AFFILIATION

Protestants are members of the dominant religion within the U.S.: for the life of the survey, 66% of the female respondents and 61% of the males indicated a preference for Protestantism. More women than men these days consider themselves to be of the Protestant persuasion: the average annual difference was a not-to-be-ignored 5.25%. More men subscribe to no religion at all (10% averaged over the last three years, compared to 6% for women).

Does Catholicism hold more of an equal appeal for men and women? Among Catholics, the annual average difference between men and women in percentage of the respective populations was much smaller...only 1.5%. Is Catholicism as appealing as it ever was? It would seem so, since the number of Catholics of either sex since the early years of the survey has hardly fluctuated. For the life of the survey, both females and males averaged a 25% Catholic response.

Comparatively on a percentage basis, lapsed female Catholics are a larger group than lapsed Protestant women, while the men were bouncing from their childhood religions at an equal pace. To the question of what religion were they raised, 29% of the female respondents answered (averaged for the life of the survey) "Catholic" and 67%, Protestant. 28% of the male respondents answered "Catholic" and 64%, Protestant. And what of the Jewish minority? Comparing the last three years of the survey to the first three, females show almost a significant drop, with 4% claiming a Jewish preference in 1972-74 and 1% in 1987-89. Men, on the other hand, were consistently in the 2 to 3% range the entire survey.

Q 1: What is your religious preference? Is it Protestant, Catholic, Jewish, some other religion, or no religion?

Responses:
PR = Protestant   CT = Catholic   JW = Jewish
NO = None   OT = Other

SEX	RESP	'72	'73	'74	'75	'76	'77	'78	'80	'82	'83	'84	'85	'86	'87	'88	'89
F	PR	67%	64%	65%	68%	65%	69%	66%	66%	68%	63%	67%	65%	67%	66%	64%	67%
	CT	24	26	26	24	27	24	27	25	25	28	25	26	25	24	27	24
	JW	3	4	4	1	2	2	1	2	3	2	1	2	2	1	2	1
	NO	3	4	4	6	6	4	6	5	4	6	5	6	4	6	5	6
	OT	2	2	1	1	0	1	1	1	1	1	1	1	2	2	2	2
# SURVEYED		804	803	793	819	829	834	886	826	866	907	867	843	847	821	842	875

SEX	RESP	'72	'73	'74	'75	'76	'77	'78	'80	'82	'83	'84	'85	'86	'87	'88	'89
M	PR	61%	61%	64%	62%	62%	63%	62%	61%	61%	59%	60%	59%	57%	64%	58%	59%
	CT	27	26	24	25	25	25	23	24	24	27	26	28	27	24	25	26
	JW	3	2	2	2	2	2	3	3	2	3	2	2	3	2	2	2
	NO	7	9	10	10	10	9	11	10	12	9	10	9	10	8	12	11
	OT	1	2	1	1	2	2	2	3	2	2	1	2	3	3	4	3
# SURVEYED		804	697	690	669	668	689	642	639	632	688	594	686	620	639	638	658

Q 2: In what religion were you raised? NOTE: Question not asked in 1972.

Responses: PR = Protestant CT = Catholic JW = Jewish
NO = None OT = Other

SEX	RESP	'73	'74	'75	'76	'77	'78	'80	'82	'83	'84	'85	'86	'87	'88	'89
F	PR	66%	65%	71%	65%	69%	67%	69%	67%	63%	68%	65%	67%	68%	65%	65%
	CT	27	28	24	29	26	28	27	26	30	27	28	27	27	28	27
	JW	3	4	1	2	2	1	2	3	3	2	2	2	1	2	2
	NO	2	3	3	3	3	3	3	2	3	3	4	2	3	3	4
	OT	2	1	1	1	1	0	1	1	0	1	1	2	1	2	2
# SURVEYED		801	791	820	830	833	886	826	865	902	862	842	847	811	843	876

SEX	RESP	'73	'74	'75	'76	'77	'78	'80	'82	'83	'84	'85	'86	'87	'88	'89
M	PR	65%	68%	67%	64%	68%	66%	65%	64%	62%	63%	62%	62%	66%	63%	60%
	CT	29	26	28	29	26	27	26	28	30	28	30	29	27	28	32
	JW	2	2	2	2	3	3	3	2	3	3	2	3	2	2	2
	NO	3	3	3	3	2	3	4	4	3	3	4	4	3	4	4
	OT	1	0	0	2	1	1	2	2	1	2	1	2	2	3	2
# SURVEYED		699	691	670	667	690	639	640	634	688	590	687	621	631	638	657

☛ The older the survey group, the more likely it was to be Protestant. For the last three years of the survey, the age blocks had the following Protestant averages: 18-35, 57%; 36-41, 61%; 42-47, 63%; 48-53, 69%; 54-59, 74%; 60-65, 72%; and 66+, 70%.

☛ Likewise, the older the group, the less likely it was to cite "none." The 18-41 displayed fairly strong, consistent figures in that area, with an average (over last three years) of a bit over 11%; in comparison, only 3.5% of the 48+ group said "none."

☛ Black respondents were overwhelmingly Protestant: 86% for the life of the survey.

No, but let me know when you see one

HAVE YOU HUGGED A PROTESTANT TODAY?

Since approximately 60% of America is Protestant, it isn't surprising that conditions are warm. For the life of the survey, an average of 63% of the women surveyed placed Protestants in the top three categories–70, 80 and 90 degrees–and even more than half (52%) of the men, those unusually stoic creatures when it comes to admitting warm feelings about religion or politics, scored in the upper regions of the scale.

Comparatively, it was the older survey participants who loved the Protestants the most: the 42+ group, for the three years surveyed, averaged some 69% in the tropical region. The 18-41 block was significantly cooler but still enthusiastic, with 48%.

Did the TV evangelist debacle precipitate a cooling spell? You betcha: the concupiscent capers of prominent Protestant figures probably account for the chilling 5% drop among women in 1988. Even the collective male thermometer dropped a point, further evidence that a cold wind was indeed a blowin' in 1988. Warmer temperatures returned in 1989, proving that those who feel kindly toward Protestants are not one to hold a grudge.

Q : **On a temperature scale from 0 to 100 how warm or cool do you feel toward Protestants.**

RELIGION ▼ DEATH

SEX	RESP	'86	'88	'89
F	00	1%	1%	0%
	10	1	1	1
	20	0	1	1
	30	1	1	1
	40	3	1	3
	50	15	27	21
	60	13	9	8
	70	20	20	19
	80	21	19	24
	90	23	20	22
# SURVEYED		801	793	531

SEX	RESP	'86	'88	'89
M	00	1%	0%	2%
	10	1	1	1
	20	1	0	1
	30	1	1	3
	40	4	3	4
	50	21	33	27
	60	20	11	11
	70	21	21	21
	80	20	16	18
	90	11	14	13
# SURVEYED		596	602	400

☛ The average annual difference between men and women during the period surveyed is 11%.

☛ The gap between men and women dropped to 8% in 1988, when women's scores dropped 5% and men's 1%.

☛ Black respondents were slightly cooler toward Protestants than whites, with a 55% response in the warmer climes. White respondents averaged 60% for the three years of the survey.

Partly sunny with a chance of rain

CATHOLIC WEATHER

Are women more hot-blooded than men about religion in general? Responses to all three questions measuring attitudes toward major religious groups suggest that men are less inclined to warm and fuzzy feelings about religion.

And what about Catholics? Three-quarters of the American people are practicing non-Catholics. Yet, despite our natural propensity to regard others—especially "different-from-us" others—with more than a modicum of circumspection (euphemism for bias), male and female responses were only a little cooler toward Catholics than they were toward Protestants. That Pope John Paul George & Ringo II is one popular guy.

Three years of tracking is not enough to monitor trends but provides fertile ground for casual observation and hypothetical wanderings. The question, first of all, asks respondents how they feel about "Catholics." Not the Catholic church. And not Catholicism. It is important to remember that, as it is important to remember where you parked your car at the mall. Women persistantly felt warmer about Catholics. The widest gap between the genders occurred in 1986, when the male/female split in attitude registered a whopping 11% divergence (measuring the warmest pro-Catholic responses by degree of warmth, on a scale from 1 to 100).

By 1988, the mercury took a nose dive for both men and women...especially for women: their warmth level dropped a full five points, with men following close on their heals with a four-point trough. Did the TV evangel-scandal affect our views of Catholics as well as Protestants? Why would men's estimation of Catholics fall more sharply than it does for Protestants?

And is it true that black patent leather shoes really do reflect up?

Q: **On a temperature scale from 0 to 100 how warm or cool do you feel toward Catholics?**
NOTE: Question was not asked in 1972-1985, 1987.

Responses: 00 = 0-9 degrees   10 = 10-19   20 = 20-29
30 = 30-39   40 = 40-49   50 = 50-59
60 = 60-69   70 = 70-79   80 = 80-89   90 = 90-99

SEX	RESP	'86	'88	'89	SEX	RESP	'86	'88	'89
F	0	1%	1%	2%	M	00	1%	2%	2%
	1	1	1	2		10	1	1	2
	2	0	0	1		20	0	0	0
	3	2	2	3		30	3	2	2
	4	5	3	4		40	8	4	5
	5	13	25	21		50	17	31	26
		17	12	9		60	20	13	15
	7	20	20	20		70	22	19	17
	8	21	20	21		80	17	15	17
	9	19	15	18		90	10	11	13
# SURVEYED		805	792	535	# SURVEYED		605	604	406

☛ Although feelings toward Catholics warmed again in 1989, men's ratings remained 2% and women 1% below the 1986 tropical spell (whereas Protestants recovered almost entirely). Sunny skies ahead for the Vatican? The weather vane will tell...

☛ The average annual difference between men's and women's feelings of warmth toward Catholics is 11%. The greatest difference occurs in 1989, with a 12% divergence.

☛ Men's ratings dropped 4% in 1988 and women's dropped 5; while women's ratings recovered all but one point the following year, men lagged 2% behind.

☛ Warmest age group? 54+, with an average of 74% registering temperatures above 60 degrees for the life of the survey. Coolest group is 18-41, with 37% measuring 59 degrees or below (for the entire survey).

Nothing more than feelings

ATTITUDE TOWARD JEWISH PEOPLE

It's no surprise that public sentiment toward religious groups, particularly the Jewish, is highly influenced by current international events. The volatility of feelings, particularly in the 50 to 70 degree range, about Jewish people over the four years surveyed suggests that current issues figure heavily in the sentiment of American men and women toward Jews. Public perception of Israeli politics can easily inflame latent anti-Semitic feelings, which probably explains the fact that Judaism is the least popular of the three religions covered on this survey.

However, the restraint which Israel displayed during the Desert Storm conflict may significantly inflate favorable survey responses in 1991. In a related survey in this book, Israel had the distinction of being the country that had lost the most favor with American men and women between 1974 and 1989.

Q: **On a temperature scale from 0 to 100 how warm or cool do you feel toward Jewish people?** NOTE: Question was not asked in 1972-1985, 1987.

Responses: 00 = 0-9 degrees | 10 = 10-19 | 20 = 20-29
30 = 30-39 | 40 = 40-49 | 50 = 50-59
60 = 60-69 | 70 = 70-79 | 80 = 80-89 | 90 = 90-99

SEX	RESP	'86	'88	'89	SEX	RESP	'86	'88	'89
F	00	2%	2%	2%	M	00	3%	2%	3%
	10	2	1	2		10	2	2	2
	20	1	1	2		20	1	1	0
	30	2	2	3		30	4	4	3
	40	6	4	6		40	8	4	6
	50	18	37	29		50	22	37	32
	60	17	12	12		60	21	13	15
	70	25	19	19		70	21	15	21
	80	18	14	14		80	12	14	12
	90	11	8	11		90	6	6	7
# SURVEYED		788	775	519	# SURVEYED		598	603	397

☛ Women, in particular, cooled their feeling for Jewish people: from 1986 to 1988, women dropped 13% in warmth of feeling toward Jews, to regain but 3% in 1989. Although male support dipped 4% by 1988, it gained 5% in 1989, so that the net effect is a 1% percent increase. The female response is interesting; when asked to rate their feelings toward Israel, women actually registered a slight positive increase, while men declined by 10%.

☛ The average annual male/female difference is 8%. Men's lowest level of sympathy toward Jews never approaches that of women.

☛ The lowest three categories accounted for not more than 6% for any year, male or female. So most of those not putting Jewish people in the highest categories were at least putting them in the 50 and 60 degree categories.

☛ Warmest (80 degrees and above) age group is the 60-65, with 59% over the life of the survey (277 polled).

In da beginning dare was da word... but whose?

INTERPRETING THE BIBLE

That more women than men support a literal interpretation of the Bible should come as no surprise since statistics indicate that women, on the whole, tend to be more religious and attracted to fundamentalism. On average, 12% more women than men chose the literal interpretation of the Good Book: that is, that the Bible is the actual word of God, to be taken word for word.

Why is this? (We're only asking.) Do women generally tend to be more literal than men? (We have no idea.) Do they interpret other religious issues with equal literalism? (See belief in an afterlife.) Are they more apt to submit wholesale to authority? (See obedience as a childhood trait.) The questions could continue until the apocalypse, at which time the three-headed beast will appear...or was that just a metaphor? (We have no idea.)

It is also intriguing to note the increasing number of men and women who believe the Bible to be an ancient book of fables and moral precepts recorded by men. And that the number of literal-minded women and men appears to be on the slide, particularly with female respondents (a drop of 7% in five years).

Q: **Which of these statements comes closest to describing your feelings about the Bible? Chose only one code.**

Responses: **AW =** The Bible is the actual word of God and is to be taken literally, word for word.

IW = The Bible is the inspired word of God but not everything should be taken literally.

AB = The Bible is an ancient book of fables, legends, history, and moral precepts recorded by men.

SEX	RESP	'84	'85	'87	'88	'89	SEX	RESP	'84	'85	'87	'88	'89
F	AW	44%	44%	43%	39%	37%	M	AW	29%	32%	31%	29%	26%
	IW	45	45	44	46	50		IW	51	53	50	50	52
	AB	10	10	13	14	12		AB	19	15	19	20	22
# SURVEYED		560	315	517	828	555	# SURVEYED		403	418	427	622	415

☛ More men than women chose the two categories other than the "Actual Word" category, with an average male/female difference of 5% for the Bible as the "inspired word of God" and an average annual difference of 7% for the Bible as "a book of fables."

☛ The 7% of female respondents who departed the literal interpretation category found the "Inspired Word" category most accommodating, with 5% finding refuge there.

☛ Compared to women, nearly twice the number of men believe the Bible to be written by men: 11% of the female respondents and 19% of the male (for the life of the survey).

☛ Black respondents were far more likely to go literal: 58% for the life of the survey.

☛ The 66+ age group was a haven for literalists: 48%, average for the life of the survey.

☛ Age group most supporting the notion of the Bible as a literary work of human origin? The 36-41, with 18% for the life of the survey.

The Big Chill

SUICIDE FOR PRIVATE REASONS

Some 30,000 adults annually take their lives, and the "suicide solution" – as an Ozzy Osbourne song calls it – has taken on a sort of cult status for a growing contingency of pop satanists. For the life of the survey, 16% of the male and 12% of the female respondents supported suicide if the respondent was properly tired of life and ready to die.

Nevertheless, more than 80% of men and women in the GSS did not believe that a person has the right to end his or her life for the above reasons. Our views haven't changed much over time: averaging the first and the last three survey years, men have fluctuated less than 1% while women varied slightly more than 1%.

Why are women more disapproving of suicide than men? Perhaps they are more apt to put themselves in the shoes of the survivors. Are they more likely to see a half full glass of water? Women may suffer more from periodic bouts of depression than men, which may lend a certain strength to their convictions. Are women more afraid of a wrong-way ticket on the Stygian ferry? Religion may play a strong role, and women, according to the GSS, are certainly more religious. Is it that typical female prerogative to lapse into morality when all about looks glum? Holding up standards of conduct seems to be a constant of female behavior.

And the contradiction between giving birth to life and watching it die by its own hand is not an easy one to resolve.

Q: **Do you think a person has the right to end his or her life if this person is tired of living and ready to die?** NOTE: Question was not asked in 1972-1976, 1979-1981, 1984, 1987.

Responses: **YES** **NO**

SEX	RESP	'77	'78	'82	'83	'85	'86	'88	'89
F	YES	11%	10%	13%	13%	11%	14%	12%	12%
	NO	89	90	87	87	89	86	88	88
# SURVEYED		820	875	830	872	822	839	531	561

SEX	RESP	'77	'78	'82	'83	'85	'86	'88	'89
M	YES	16%	15%	17%	18%	15%	17%	13%	16%
	NO	84	85	83	82	85	83	87	84
# SURVEYED		676	636	622	677	673	607	423	419

☞ As many as 18% of the men (1983) and 14% of the women (1986) agreed that suicide might be okay if you're bored and depressed.

☞ As many as 90% of the women (1978) and 87% (1988) thought it'd be a better idea to read a dull book and whine.

☞ Black and white respondents are in essential agreement on suicide for private reasons, with 13% of the black and 14% of the white respondents supporting the idea.

☞ Averaging the entire survey period for various age groups, the most positive response is found among the 18-23s: a full 16% voted thumbs up. Interestingly, a steady decline in approval occurs from 30 to 65. But the renegade 66+, many nearer to death than thee, jump 3% from the previous age group to a 13% approval.

☞ The mean approval for all respondents was 14%.

Suicide is not painless...

TERMINALLY ILL HAVE THE RIGHT TO STOP LIVING?

A 1990 *USA Today* survey of 724 adults revealed that 68% of the respondents believe circumstances exist in which a person with a terminal illness should be allowed to commit suicide.

The results of the General Social Survey indicate that both sexes are becoming more tolerant of suicide for the terminally ill. In 1977-78, male respondents averaged a 44% and females 36% approval for the right of the terminally ill to commit suicide. By 1988-89, that approval had increased to 56% for males and 47% for females. In the '80s, their sympathies were likely touched by AIDS and Alzheimer's, two diseases with no cures and plenty of suffering.

While the medical profession still cannot cure much of what ails us, it often can sustain us – and merely sustain us – to the point where one is sometimes forced to question whether life is being preserved or death protracted. The precept of the Hemlock Society, to which some 28,000 members belong, is that the severely ill have the right to end their lives. In 1980, the Vatican determined that refusing treatment for the terminally ill is "acceptance of the human condition," and recent years have seen the proliferation of living wills, specifying what sort of treatment is unacceptable in the case of terminal illness. But these wills do not provide for those who have long-term debilitating illnesses, such as Alzheimer's.

Perhaps the ever-eroding taboo against discussion of euthanasia and medically assisted suicide was dealt another blow by the celebrated case of Jack Kevorkian, a retired pathologist in Pontiac, Michigan, whose so-called "suicide machine" aided the 1990 death of Alzheimer-stricken Janet Adkins. 43% of the respondents to that *USA Today* poll cited above believed that Dr. Kevorkian should not be punished for his role in aiding the death of Adkins, and only 19% believed he should lose his medical license. And perhaps most telling: a full 65% believed that medical facilities should be available for the terminally ill to end their lives.

Eventually, murder charges against Kevorkian, dubbed "Dr. Death" by the press, were dismissed, although he has been barred from using his suicide machine. Just prior to Adkins news-making death, a poll was completed by the Times Mirror Center for the People and the Press, revealing that 49% of the respondents believed that incurably ill patients have a moral right to commit suicide. An extra 6% believed that if great pain was involved, the moral right existed. 80% thought that the right to die should be allowed in some circumstances.

As for our survey, an average 9% gap exists between men and women on this issue, with 1986 showing a 15% spread. Why the difference? Men commit suicide at a rate two to three times that of women, so perhaps men and women have considerably different opinions on "quality of life." Women may be more inclined to hold on to the religious and moral viewpoint that suicide is wrong, whatever the circumstances.

At any rate, both men and women are much more inclined to favor euthanasia laws over suicide for the terminally ill – by an average of some 20% – which might lead to some interesting questions about how we feel about the role of the medical profession in suicide for the terminally ill...

Q: **Do you think a person has the right to end his or her life if this person has an incurable disease?** NOTE: Question was not asked in 1972-1976, 1979-1981, 1984, 1987.

Responses: **YES** **NO**

SEX	RESP	'77	'78	'82	'83	'85	'86	'88	'89
F	YES	36%	36%	43%	46%	42%	47%	49%	45%
	NO	64	64	57	54	58	53	51	55
# SURVEYED		803	860	815	863	816	822	523	544

SEX	RESP	'77	'78	'82	'83	'85	'86	'88	'89
M	YES	43%	44%	53%	54%	50%	62%	56%	55%
	NO	57	56	47	46	50	38	44	45
# SURVEYED		672	623	615	667	664	598	423	413

☛ While 54% of the white respondents over the last three survey years supported suicide for the terminally ill, only 36% of the black respondents did.

☛ What a difference a generation or two makes. Age group most in favor of suicide for the terminally ill was the 30-35, with 64% during the last three survey years. Least in favor was the 66+, at 35%.

Pulling the plug

SHOULD EUTHANASIA BE ALLOWED?

Euthanasia – literally meaning "easy death" – is a subject of much debate in these days of life-supporting technologies never dreamt of by the Greeks. Right-to-die activists are becoming an increasing presence in this imbroglio of medical, legal, and ethical questions. Science forces us constantly to reexamine our definition of life, and we are faced with questions and decisions which have never before been the burden of society.

And don't forget, the boomers, 70 million plus, are aging. What happens when they, as a group, run into the usual assortment of health problems associated with old age? The Pepsi generation becomes the pacemaker generation?

Those who believe that no "right to die" exists are a dwindling minority: in 1977, 38%, and in 1989 only 31% of our respondents condemned euthanasia, a trend reflected among both sexes.

During the first three survey years, 66% of the male and 59% of the female respondents supported the concept of euthanasia. The Karen Anne Quinlan situation was in the news. Quinlan had lapsed into a coma in 1975, and her parents battled in the court for several years for permission to disconnect her life support system. This was the first major case where medical technology clearly streaked past human ethical judgement, a trend in the making.

By the last three survey years, 74% of the male and 65% of the female respondents supported euthanasia. Between the 1975 Quinlan case and 1990, 50 courts in 17 states have considered the right of a patient's family to have treatment withdrawn. And justice has been merciful for those who have taken upon themselves, without the blessing of the law, the role of mercy killer: of 20 cases of mercy killing in the past 50 years, only 3 defendants were sentenced to jail.

A 1990 *Time*/CNN poll found that 80% of the respondents felt that if a patient is terminally ill and unconscious but has left instructions in a living will, the doctor should be allowed to withdraw life-sustaining treatment. 57% thought that situations existed in which doctors could administer lethal drugs.

In a poll conducted in 1990 for the *National Law Journal,* 800 respondents were asked who should decide to end artificial life support. 1% said the court, 8% the doctor, and a whopping 88% said the family should decide. And a poll published in 1990 in the *Detroit Free Press* indicated that 62% of respondents believed that they could make the decision to end life-support for a comatose relative with virtually no chance of recovery. 51% of the 1,000 persons queried said the family has the right to remove life support, while 26% believed that life support should only be interrupted if the patient has previously indicated such a preference. Only 9% would leave it to the doctors, and just 7% would allow the machines to continue running without consideration.

The University of Colorado and the San Francisco Medical Society conducted surveys which illuminate how doctors feel about so-called mercy killing. In separate studies of doctors' attitudes toward euthanasia (published in 1988), they found that at least 60% of physicians feel that patients should have the option of choosing when to die. At least 35% would practice euthanasia if it were legal. And how about this for an eye-opener: more than 36% of the doctors surveyed have administered medication for pain knowing it would hasten the patient's death. Is it time to amend the Hippocratic oath? ("I will give no deadly medicine to anyone if asked, nor suggest any such counsel...")

Q: **When a person has a disease that cannot be cured, do you think doctors should be allowed by law to end the patient's life by some painless means if the patient and his family request it?** NOTE: Question was not asked in 1972-1976, 1979-1981, 1984, 1987.

Responses: YES   NO

SEX	RESP	'77	'78	'82	'83	'85	'86	'88	'89
F	YES	58%	57%	61%	62%	62%	64%	66%	64%
	NO	42	43	39	38	38	36	34	36
# SURVEYED		787	851	819	860	815	819	519	543
SEX	RESP	'77	'78	'82	'83	'85	'86	'88	'89
M	YES	67%	64%	68%	71%	70%	74%	74%	75%
	NO	33	36	32	29	30	26	26	25
# SURVEYED		666	620	611	664	674	594	416	414

☛ Comparing the first and the last three years of the survey, we find 8% more men and 5% more women approving of euthanasia.

☛ The most supportive age groups were the 18-23 and the 24-29, with a mean positive response of just over 74%. Will they consistently hold these views into old age? Time will tell.

☛ For the last three survey years, 71% of the white respondents approved of euthanasia. Black respondents were less approving of euthanasia, at 51%.

And I can see for miles too

ESP: CONTACTING PEOPLE FAR AWAY

The female the more intuitive sex? At least they're far more likely to claim an extra-sensory experience than men. For the three years of the survey, the average for females who often or occasionally had been in touch with someone far, far away without using a telephone or the postal system (no semaphore, either) was 37%. Male respondents averaged 25%. No particular age group stands out as having better transmission lines; the figures are generally similar, routinely fluctuating 5 to 10% from year to year.

Q: **Have you ever felt as though you were in touch with someone when they were far away from you?** NOTE: Question was not asked in 1972-1983, 1985-1987.

RELIGION ▼ DEATH

SEX	RESP	'84	'88	'89	SEX	RESP	'84	'88	'89
F	NV	29%	31%	38%	M	NV	40%	41%	47%
	ON	26	35	30		ON	32	36	30
	SV	33	24	23		SV	22	19	19
	OF	12	11	8		OF	6	4	5
# SURVEYED		852	829	571	# SURVEYED		587	627	421

☛ Older folks more likely to use the telephone: the 66+ age group had the highest percentage (44%) claiming that this ESP thing had never happened to them.

☛ Black respondents had keen extra senses, with 36% claiming occasional or frequent experiences.

☛ White respondents averaged 31%.

Fear of flying?

OUT-OF-BODY EXPERIENCES

More women (19%) than men (17%) claim to have been occasionally or frequently lifted out of their bodies by a strong spiritual force. More men (62%) than women (60%) say they are not a part of the frequent flyer club. The same percentage of women (21%) and men (21%) revealed that once, just once, did occur the unusual experience of being lifted outside their corporeal entities, where they chatted amiably with a big and mighty spirit before returning to the more mundane world of microwaves and space walks.

Among age groups, travel outside the body is more likely as the group ages (and of course, finances improve). This makes sense; experience (inside and outside the body) deepens with age. Among the 18-23 group, for instance, only 13% had experienced occasional or frequent journeys outside the body. Trips to the 7-Eleven were ruled out as evidence of out-of-body experiences. At the other end of the age spectrum, 22% of the +66 group had gone for long walks with great spirits at least several times. Another 19% had experienced the sensation once.

Q: **Have you ever felt as though you were very close to a powerful, spiritual force that seemed to lift you out of yourself?** NOTE: Question was not asked in 1972-1982, 1985-1987.

RELIGION ▼ DEATH

SEX	RESP	'83	'84	'88	'89
F	NV	42%	58%	68%	72%
	ON	29	20	18	17
	SV	18	15	9	6
	OF	12	7	4	5
# SURVEYED		877	855	827	566

SEX	RESP	'83	'84	'88	'89
M	NV	49%	62%	69%	68%
	ON	26	21	19	19
	SV	16	12	8	9
	OF	9	6	5	4
# SURVEYED		662	587	624	422

☞ In 1988-89, the figures for out-of-body travel drop significantly for both men and women, perhaps in reaction to higher gasoline prices and the falling of the Berlin Wall.

☞ For the fours years charted, nearly twice the percentage of black respondents (30%, 607 surveyed) than white (17%, 4,648 surveyed) had experienced occasional or frequent instances of out-of-body wanderings.

I feel like I've been here before

DÉJÀ VU: DÉJÀ VU: DÉJÀ VU

So how does one explain that women are more likely to use ESP and men have more frequent bouts of *déjà vu?* Gender specialization? For the life of the survey, 38% of the male respondents had occasional or frequent instances of *déjà vu*, compared to 36% of the females. Of course, *déjà vu* is also known scientifically as paramnesia, which is defined as an illusion of remembering scenes and events when experienced for the first time. So it may be that men are slightly more delusional, while women are more apt to experience out-of-body traveling, something many men would never try for fear of loosing their parking space.

Q : **How often have you had any of the following experiences? Thought you were somewhere you had been before, but knew that it was impossible?** NOTE: Question was not asked in 1972-1983, 1985-1987.

Responses: NV = Never in my life   ON = Once in my life;
SV = Several times   OF = Often

SEX	RESP	'84	'88	'89
F	NV	35%	33%	40%
	ON	23	33	29
	SV	31	27	24
	OF	11	7	7
# SURVEYED		851	827	567

SEX	RESP	'84	'88	'89
M	NV	31%	33%	32%
	ON	30	32	30
	SV	31	30	32
	OF	8	6	7
# SURVEYED		588	629	423

☛ In theory, the youngest age groups should have more of a tendency to feel like they been somewhere they've never been to, since they're not as well traveled. And it's true: the older you get the more likely you are to feel like you've already been here before, because you've already been here before. For the life of the survey, 47% of the 18-29 age group (972 surveyed) occasionally or frequently had deja vu experiences, while only 16% of the +66 age group did (653 surveyed).

☛ More women than men have never had the experience: 36% of the females and 32% of the males say it never happened to them.

Reach out and touch someone...

IN TOUCH WITH THE DEAD

Question: What do Ouija boards, past-life therapy, chan-neling, and Shirley MacLaine have in common? Answer: That '80s-style new ageism that aspires to "plug into a higher circuitry."   All sorts of crystal-sporting new agers these days are a-buzz with talk about reincarnation and rap sessions with discarnate beings (channeled spirits, unlike the ones that come from the cable box).

And how about that *Ghost* movie, that topped the charts for weeks and grossed $212 million in no time. Seems like people are talking about the dead, but are they talking to the dead? Not according to our survey. Over the three years surveyed, an average of more than 60% of our respon-dents had never been in touch with the dead. Men are even less likely than women to have ever made such con-tact: 66% of the men, as opposed to 56% of the women, on average, have never been in touch with someone who had died. Perhaps they just send flowers.

But wait a minute. For the life of the survey, 20% of the female respondents have had occasional or frequent con-tact with dead people! This is a sizeable number of both living and dead people gabbing if one takes into account the U.S. population as a whole. We're talking millions! The energy within the universe is a constant, never expanding or contracting. Who's to say we can't feel a spirit? Not us. The great beyond may be just beyond.

Q: **Have you ever felt as though you were really in touch with someone who had died.** NOTE: Question was not asked in 1972-1983, 1985-1987.

Responses: NV = Never in my life   ON = Once in my life
SV = Several times   OF = Often

SEX	RESP	'86	'88	'89
F	NV	53%	56%	60%
	ON	24	24	24
	SV	17	13	10
	OF	6	7	6
# SURVEYED		857	831	569

SEX	RESP	'86	'88	'89
M	NV	64%	66%	70%
	ON	23	25	21
	SV	10	6	6
	OF	3	4	3
# SURVEYED		588	628	422

☛ The trend among both men and women is away from after-death communication: 6% more men and 7% more women responded "Never" in touch with the dead in the last year versus the first year of the survey. Doesn't MCI have a special long-distance rate?

☛ Women were, on average, 10% more apt to have been in touch with someone who had died. And they stay in touch: while men and women average about the same in the "once" category, women come out 10% ahead of men in the "several times" category and 3% ahead in the "often" category. Haven't they always said women communicate better?

☛ Black respondents were more likely to speak with the dead than white respondents, with 21% of the black respondents occasionally or frequently in contact, compared to 15% of the white respondents.

☛ Does age make a difference in your ability to contact the dead? Yup. Probably because more folks are gone who you miss and wouldn't mind chatting with. The 66+ age group averaged 24% who occasionally or frequently were in touch with a dead person, compared to 9% of the 18-23 block.

No, but I once saw a moose through a pair of binoculars

EVER EXPERIENCED SECOND SIGHT, SIXTH SENSE?

Of all the paranormal states discussed here, seeing events at a great distance as they occur seems to be more on a par with travel to Alaska: both are states infrequently visited. The percentages for females and males are very similar, with the great majority of both sexes (74% female, 72% male) claiming never to have enjoyed such spectacular vision. If such an experience does occur, it appears to be a once-in-a-lifetime event for most, the extrasensory equivalent to a hole-in-one on the 375-yard 9th hole.

The small percentage (3%) of males and females who claim to have such visions often leads to less than intriguing questions: does seeing events at a great distance get in the way of more mundane tasks like driving and shaving? Or is the experience like one of those split-vision television screens? Is the vision always something important or are many of them routine, like being able to sit at home and see a guy who lives three blocks away taking the trash out? Or if the events often involve strangers whose name and location are unknown, wouldn't that get irritating?

Q: **Have you ever seen events that happened at a great distance as they were happening?** NOTE: Question was not asked in 1972-1983, 1985-1987.

SHE SAID HE SAID

Responses: NV = Never in my life   ON = Once in my life;
SV = Several times   OF = Often

SEX	RESP	'84	'88	'89
F	NV	70%	73%	78%
	ON	18	17	14
	SV	9	7	6
	OF	3	3	2
# SURVEYED		852	819	561

SEX	RESP	'84	'88	'89
M	NV	70%	70%	75%
	ON	18	18	15
	SV	9	9	8
	OF	2	4	2
# SURVEYED		582	621	422

☛ Once past the age of 60, the ability to see events far away seems to diminish (and many complain that it's often harder to see things close-up, too). The average for the +60 crowd that had experienced a second sight sensation at least once was 20%, compared to 38% for the 18-23 age bracket.

☛ Black respondents were more likely than whites to have had the sensation: 43% (441 surveyed for the three years) had experienced such a vision at least once, compared to 25% (3,267 total) of the whites polled.